New Piano Series

STUDENT GUIDE 7

Canadian Cataloguing in Publication Data
Main entry under title:
New piano series : student guide : a guide to the study of The Royal Conservatory of Music... examination repertoire = un guide pour le repertoire d'examen du Royal Conservatory of Music

ISBN 0-88797-462-7 (set)
ISBN 0-88797-452-X (v. 7)

1. Piano — Instruction and study.
I. Royal Conservatory of Music.

MT245.N48 1994 786.2'07 C94-930562-6

FREDERICK HARRIS MUSIC

A Guide to the Study of the Examination Repertoire of The Royal Conservatory of Music - Grade 7
Un guide pour le répertoire d'examen du Royal Conservatory of Music - Niveau 7

PREFACE

The Student Guides are designed to accompany the Piano Repertoire Albums of the *New Piano Series*. They have been created for students to help them develop a deeper understanding of, and interest in, the repertoire being studied.

The text and examples were written by distinguished musicians, including faculty members of The Royal Conservatory of Music. The following team of authors, teachers, and editors was instrumental in the creation of the Student Guides: Mildred Bennett, Elaine Capper, Anne Cumming, Robin Elliott, John Gaspar, Eugene Gates, Monica Gaylord, Susan Hamblin, Carla Hartsfield, Aasta Levene, Lynda Metelsky, and Ruth Pincoe.

Each Student Guide contains a series of one-page articles which summarize the most important features of each piece in the Piano Repertoire Album for the respective grade. Each article includes 1) a short biographical sketch of the composer; 2) a description of the form and content of the piece; and 3) an explanation of technical challenges and practice tips. The discussion is selective; much more could be said about these works.

Musical examples in the Student Guides are excerpts or fragments only. At all times, the student should use the Guide side by side with the complete piece of music.

The Glossary at the back of each Student Guide gives brief explanations of the technical terms and expressions. These terms are highlighted in the text when they first appear in each article (for example, ***motive***). Students should refer to a standard theory text for explanations of basic rudiments (names of the notes, intervals, scales, etc.).

The Introduction includes material generally applicable to most of the repertoire (for example, how to play *staccato*). The authors recommend that the student refer to the Introduction, as well as reading through the individual articles.

In general, the text has been written for the student to read independently. In addition, teachers can add significant benefit to the student's learning experience through discussion of specific topics. Parents can also enrich their child's practice sessions through shared knowledge.

The creators of the *New Piano Series* trust that users of the Student Guides will discover a heightened enjoyment and success in their study of the piano, and that these Guides will stimulate interest in further explorations of the composers and their works.

Dr. Trish Sauerbrei
Managing Editor

TABLE OF CONTENTS

INTRODUCTION

HOW TO PRACTISE

Study the Music

Study the music before you begin. Look for repetitions of rhythms, melodies, and whole measures or phrases. The more you understand about the ***harmony***, rhythm and structure, the easier it will be to learn the notes.

Practise in Sections

- Work in small sections, hands separately. (Each section should overlap the next by a few notes.)
- Learn the ***articulation*** and dynamics as you learn the notes.
- Use the given fingering. If you run into a problem, you can work out a different fingering that suits your hand better. Write this fingering in your music and use it every time.
- Begin working hands together in small sections. Play slowly and listen to the balance of sound between your hands.

Tips for Practising

- Play with firm fingers. Place each finger in the very centre of the key.
- Make sure the fast passages are even. When you play fast passages with both hands, the notes should sound exactly together.
- Learn the notes and the phrasing of each hand before you play hands together.
- Practise similar measures and sections together.
- Close the piano and practise on the wood. Focus on fingering and articulation.

Shadow or Ghost Practising

Move your fingers over the notes as if you were playing the piece, but don't press down the keys. This will help you to work out leaps and finger changes. It will also help you to memorize the piece. Shadow both hands separately, then play one hand and shadow the other.

Memory

Rely on more than your "motor memory." Focus on harmony, melodic intervals, fingering, and the visual image of the page.

- Choose key passages and learn them from every possible angle.
- Practise losing your spot! Then jump ahead to one of these signpost passages.
- Know the final key of the piece!

Italian Words

Look up the meanings of Italian terms in a music dictionary, and write them in your music. This will help you to acquire a musical vocabulary.

Technique

Technique is your friend, but most students treat technical work like a friend who lives far away – one that you hardly ever see. A solid grounding in technique is the basis for security and expertise at the keyboard.

- When you play scales, concentrate on smoothness and speed.
- Practise scales at slow, medium and fast tempos.
- Practise scales in rhythms (quarters, eighths, triplets, then sixteenths).
- Practise scales with different touches, such as *staccato, portato,* and short slurs (two or three notes).

DYNAMICS

There is a range of volume and intensity within any dynamic level. Create subtle shadings within each level.

- Make little peaks within phrases.
- Taper the volume at phrase endings.
- Shape a rising and falling melody with small *crescendos* and *diminuendos*.
- The ***dominant*** chord carries more tension than the ***tonic***. Play it with a little more intensity.

Playing Pianissimo

The volume of sound depends on the speed with which the finger presses the key down. *Pianissimo* playing requires a slower finger action, even in rapid passagework.

- Press the keys down very slowly and gently. Keep the tone as even as possible.
- Keep your fingers in contact with the keys.

ARTICULATION AND TONE

Articulation

Articulation is a term used to describe the way you play the notes – *legato, staccato,* detached, *tenuto, portato, marcato*, etc. These different touches depend on detailed control of your fingers, hand and wrist.

Staccato

Practise your *staccato* technique in both hands.

- Release the notes quickly.
- Keep your fingers close to the keys.
- Pull your fingers in toward your palm as you lift off the keys.

A Full, Legato Sound

- Listen carefully to each note you play.
- Connect the sound of each note to the next. (Remember to lift at the end of the slurs.)
- Keep your arms and hands relaxed and your wrists flexible.
- Feel the weight of your arm behind each finger. Transfer this weight evenly from finger to finger.
- Play on the fleshy pads of your fingers rather than on your fingertips. Sink into the keys. Press each one down to the keybed.

Repeated Notes

- Change fingers on repeated notes. Why? When you change fingers you change the balance of your hand. This gives a more varied tone. (Repeated notes played with one finger sound like tapping.)
- To practise repeated notes, try this exercise:

HINT: If there is a lot of repetition in the piece, varied articulation in both hands will lend interest and vitality to the music. Think about which notes you want to play slurred or detached.

Triplets

To get accustomed to the triplet rhythm, try this clapping exercise:

To switch to triplets and back again, clap these rhythms. Set your metronome at a comfortable speed. Each click will be an eighth note.

Trills

- Play ***trills*** lightly.
- Use precise, economical finger movements.
- Keep your hand, wrist and arm in constant motion. Flexibility is the key to successful trills.
- Let the tempo of the music guide the length of the trills. The slower the tempo, the longer the trill and the more notes you should play.

ACCOMPANIMENT

Alberti Bass

The ***Alberti bass*** was named after Domenico Alberti (1710 - *ca*1740), an Italian singer, harpsichordist and composer who used this figure extensively in his keyboard compositions.

To Practise an Alberti Bass

(You can also use these exercises to practise any regular accompaniment pattern.)

1. Play each group of four notes as a solid chord. Use the correct fingering.
2. Practise with a *staccato* or a *portato* touch.
3. Practise in dotted rhythms.

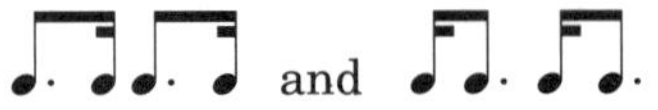

4. Practise with different accent patterns.

5. Play all the notes doubled.

HINT: You can often use the steady beat of an *Alberti-bass* accompaniment to co-ordinate the rhythms in the R.H. melody.

Balance the Accompaniment

Give the melody a stronger sound than the accompaniment. Keep the accompaniment about two dynamic levels softer. For example, if the marking is *mezzo forte*, play the accompaniment *piano*. If the marking is *forte*, play the accompaniment *mezzo piano*.

To achieve a good balance between melody and accompaniment, play the melody line at a normal volume while silently touching the keys of the accompanying part. Gradually increase the pressure on the notes of the accompanying part until the notes sound faintly.

THE PEDAL

The right, damper pedal enhances the sound. The overtones it sets up give an extra bloom to the notes.

Legato pedalling:

- Time your pedal changes carefully. (As a rule of thumb, pedal each chord change.)
- Lift your foot up and quickly press it down immediately after the note or chord sounds to catch the chord cleanly.
- Use your ear to judge the timing of your pedalling. Listen carefully to the effect you produce.

Pedal Exercise

1. Play a scale with one finger. Pedal each note to achieve a good *legato*.
2. Now play the scale with triads. (Use root position for the L.H. and first inversion for the R.H.) Pedal each chord.

Pedal and Balance of Sound

- Play the music hands together without the pedal. Experiment until you find a good balance of sound.
- When you add the pedal, make sure it enhances the balance of sound.
- Pedal only as deeply as you need to get the desired sound. Use half-pedalling for a lighter sound. Use a deeper pedal to intensify the sound.

CIRCLE OF 5THS

The circle of 5ths is a term used to describe the arrangement of the twelve keys in order of ascending 5ths. After twelve steps, the original key occurs again:

C	(no sharps or flats)
G	(1 sharp)
D	(2 sharps)
A	(3 sharps)
E	(4 sharps)
B	(5 sharps)
F sharp	(6 sharps) or G flat (6 flats)
C sharp	(7 sharps) or D flat (5 flats)
A flat	(4 flats)
E flat	(3 flats)
B flat	(2 flats)
F	(1 flat)
C	(no sharps or flats)

PIANO REPERTOIRE

Your *Grade 7 Piano Repertoire Album* is divided into three sections or lists.

- **List A** includes a selection of pieces composed during the Baroque period (*ca* 1600 to *ca* 1750).
  Baroque composers include Johann Sebastian Bach, Georg Philipp Telemann and Domenico Scarlatti.
- **List B** includes a selection of pieces composed during the Classical period (*ca* 1750 to *ca* 1820) as well as pieces composed in the Classical style during the 19th century.
  Classical composers include Franz Joseph Haydn and Wolfgang Amadeus Mozart.
- **List C** includes a selection of pieces from the Romantic era (*ca* 1820 to *ca* 1910) as well as from the 20th century.
  Romantic composers include Frédéric Chopin and Johannes Brahms.
  Twentieth-century composers include Béla Bartók, Witold Lutosławski and Pierre Gallant.

THE BAROQUE

Baroque Music

Baroque keyboard instruments (for example, the clavichord or the harpsichord) did not have the range of dynamics that the modern piano enjoys today. Composers would often add extra notes to a two- or three-voice piece to create a *crescendo*.

Some Baroque harpsichords had two keyboards. Performers could shift back and forth between manuals to vary the sound.

Terraced Dynamics

On most Baroque keyboard instruments, such as the harpsichord, it was not possible to control dynamic levels with finger pressure. For this reason, long sweeping *crescendos* and *diminuendos* are not part of Baroque keyboard music. Instead, Baroque musicians used terraced dynamics – abrupt shifts in volume up or down a level, rather like shifting gears. (It was possible to vary the dynamics slightly on the clavichord, however, because of the different type of action.)

Baroque Performance Practice

In the Baroque period, composers did not always write signs to indicate touch or ***ornaments*** in their music. Baroque performers were expected to add their own articulation and ornaments.

Modern editors often add dynamics and articulation marks to Baroque music. There is no single correct way to approach articulation in Baroque music. Different performers often have different opinions about touch.

You should feel free to create your own interpretation of the Baroque pieces you play, provided that you stay within the style of the period. Baroque pieces differ widely in character. Give each piece a distinct personality through your choice of articulation.

Try to listen to recordings of Baroque keyboard music. Get a copy of the music so you can follow along.

DANCES AND OTHER FORMS

A **fantasia** is an imaginative composition. It may be structured or free in its form, and is often composed in an improvisational style.

The **gavotta** (or **gavotte**) is a dance of French origin. It is usually in a duple metre with four-measure phrases beginning halfway through the measure. (The word *gavotte* is said to be derived from Gavots – inhabitants of the Pays de Gap in Dauphine, a region of France.)

The **minuet** was a fashionable and popular dance in Europe from the mid-17th century until the end of the 18th century. It has three beats to the measure, with no upbeat. It is a graceful dance in a moderate tempo, performed with balance and control. The name is said to come from the French word "menu" (small) because the dance steps are small. This dance is known as **menuet** in French, **menuett** in German, and **minuetto** in Italian.

In Bach's time, a **prelude** was usually an introduction for other works such as a suite or a fugue.

The **sarabande** is a slow dance in triple metre with an emphasis on the second beat and no upbeat. It probably originated in Mexico and appeared in Spain in the early 16th century. It appeared in France and England about 1600.

A **scherzo** is a musical joke. It has a quick 3/4 metre (like a fast waltz); a vigorous rhythm; a playful character; surprises and abrupt changes. Usually a scherzo has a contrasting Trio section with a more lyrical nature, after which the scherzo is repeated.

The difference between a minuet and a scherzo is not always clear. Haydn used the title *scherzo* for movements which were similar in style to a minuet. Beethoven introduced scherzos to replace the minuet as the third movement of sonatas, symphonies and quartets.

The **waltz** probably grew out of other triple-metre dances such as the German Dance and the *Ländler*. The development of the waltz in the 19th century was principally due to Joseph Lanner, Johann Strauss, and Johann Strauss the Younger (composer of *The Blue Danube*). Schubert, Weber, Chopin and Brahms also composed sets of waltzes.

LITTLE PRELUDE IN D MINOR
BWV 935

List A: pp. 4-5

JOHANN SEBASTIAN BACH (1685-1750)

Bach was one of the great teachers of the Baroque era. He had many pupils over the years, including the composers Johann Philipp Kirnberger and Johann Ludwig Krebs. Bach also taught music to his children; four of them became well-known composers. Bach's pupils often lived in his household and helped him out by copying music, as well as performing under his direction. Much of Bach's keyboard music, including twenty or so little preludes, was written for teaching purposes. Some of these preludes survive only in copies made by Bach's pupils.

The Opening Motive

This entire prelude is based on the six-note ***motive*** in the opening measure. The B section opens with a mirror image of the opening theme.

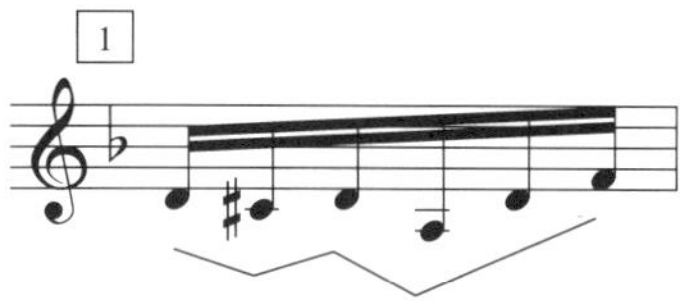

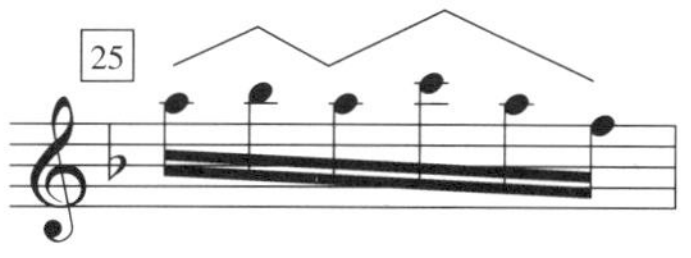

Compare these motives. What makes them different? How are they similar? Look through the music to find all the ***variations*** of this motive.

Counterpoint

A texture of two (or more) equal voices, each with its own melody, is called ***counterpoint***. Study the individual voices as you practise hands separately. Listen for these voices when you play hands together.

- Your choice of dynamics and ***articulation*** will help you to project each voice clearly.
- Bring out each important statement of the motive, using the same dynamic shape and articulation.
- Keep a sensitive balance between the hands. Don't drown out the melody in the other voice.

HINT: Play the eighth notes softer than the sixteenth notes.

Sixteenth Notes

Use a metronome when you practise. It will help you keep a steady beat.

- Plan your fingering for the broken chords and scale passages. Find a comfortable fingering and use it every time.
- Pay special attention to passages with sixteenth notes in both hands (mm. 21, 31-32, 37, 40, and 45). Practise these measures alone.

Articulation

In Baroque music, eighth notes are often shortened or detached. A mixture of detached notes and slurs will add variety and interest.

- In mm. 5-8, play the L.H. notes *portato*.
- In mm. 9-12, add a slur to the first two eighth notes of each measure. Play the R.H. sixteenth notes *legato* or use a combination of slurs and *staccatos*.

Imitation and Sequences

Rhythmic and melodic figures based on the opening measures are passed from hand to hand and repeated at different pitches.

- The opening theme in the R.H., mm. 1-2, is ***imitated*** by the L.H., mm. 3-4 and 40-43.
- The descending theme in the R.H., mm. 25-27, is imitated by the L.H., mm. 29-31.
- Bach also spins out his six-note motive with ***sequences***. The R.H. figure in m. 9 is repeated in a sequence in mm. 10-12. These four measures are imitated in the L.H., mm. 13-16.
- There is another sequence in the R.H., mm. 33-36.

Form and Keys

This piece is in ***binary form***:

A mm. 1-24
B mm. 25-48

- The A section opens in D minor. The music passes through F major and B flat major, and ends with a ***perfect cadence*** in F major.
- The B section begins in F major. The F sharp and E flat in m. 29 signal a ***modulation*** to G minor.
- In m. 37, Bach uses a broken G minor triad as a ***pivot*** to return to D minor. This triad (G-B flat-D) is the ***tonic*** of G minor and the ***subdominant*** of D minor.
- In mm. 39-40, there is a perfect cadence (V-I) in D minor and the opening theme is played by the L.H.

FANTASIA IN B FLAT MAJOR
TWV 33:18

List A: pp. 6-7

GEORG PHILIPP TELEMANN (1681-1767)

Telemann was born in Magdeburg. He studied law and modern languages at the University in Leipzig, but he had only rudimentary musical training. As a composer, he was mostly self-taught. Telemann held various posts as church music director. From 1721 until his death, he was the town musical director of Hamburg. Telemann was a prolific composer, and he engraved most of his published works himself. In 1732-1733, he published a collection of three dozen keyboard fantasias. This lively piece is the second movement of Fantasia No. 6 *from the second dozen. It is preceded by a slow introduction and followed by a short, fast dance.*

Melody

- The R.H. plays a cheerful melody with simple eighth- and sixteenth-note rhythms and a few ***ornaments***. The L.H. counter-melody moves mainly by step in eighth notes. Play the L.H. at a lower dynamic level, but use a firm touch.
- Let the R.H. sixteenth-note passages sparkle. Play them evenly, but vary your touch.
- Lift off each key as you play the next note. Keep your fingers curved. This will add clarity to the sixteenth-note passages.
- In mm. 19-21 and 23-25, bring out the lower R.H. melody notes and play the repeated Gs and Fs softly. Keep your fifth finger close to the key and hold the other fingers a little higher. Project the L.H. in these measures to emphasize the duet in 3rds between the voices.

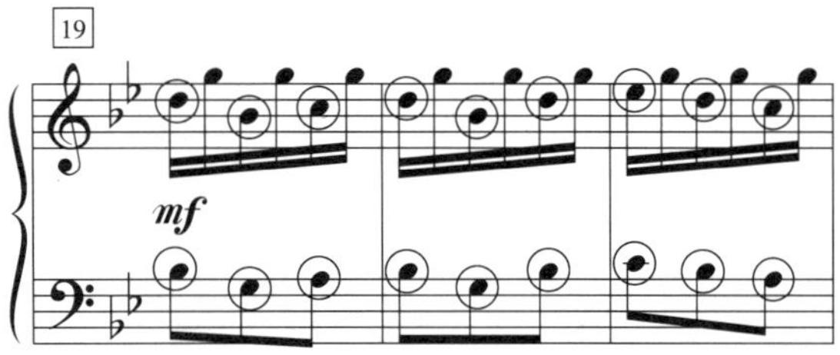

Ornaments

Fit the ***trills*** smoothly into the melody. Begin each one on the beat. Make a slight *diminuendo* through the trill and play the last note lightly. For a crisp, clear sound, keep your fingers on the keys and pull each finger slightly toward your palm as you play the note.

Adding Dynamic Colour

- Change dynamics from note to note when you play repeated notes. For example, make a small *crescendo* through the repeated B flats in mm. 2-3, 6-7, and similar passages.
- ***Chromatic*** movement adds musical tension. Enhance this by stressing altered notes such as the E natural in m. 14. The D flat in m. 55 introduces a ***harmonic*** change. Play it gently, but with a full tone.
- Play repetitions at a lower dynamic level. For example, play mm. 1-4 *mezzo forte*, as marked. Make the repeat (mm. 5-8) *mezzo piano*. Similarly, reduce the dynamic level from *piano* in mm. 55-58 to *pianissimo* in mm. 59-62.

Form

This piece is in ***rondo form***. A recurring theme in B flat major alternates with related material in other keys.

A mm. 1-18 (B flat major)
B mm. 19-36 (F major)
A mm. 37-54 (B flat major)
C mm. 55-72 (B flat minor and G minor)
A mm. 1-18 (B flat major)

Da Capo al Fine

- The first time through, play mm. 1-18 with a steady beat. Make a strong *crescendo* in m. 72 to lead back to the repeat of the opening theme.
- When you repeat mm. 1-18, make a small *ritardando* in mm. 16-17, and hold the B flat in m. 18 for its full three beats.

Modulations and Sequences

Telemann uses a ***pivot chord*** to ***modulate*** from B flat major to F major.

- The G minor triad implied in m. 22 is both the ***submediant*** (VI) of B flat major and the ***supertonic*** (II) of F major.
- In fact, mm. 19-22 are centred around a G minor chord, and mm. 23-26 are centred around an F major chord. The E natural in m. 29 confirms the modulation to F major.
- Did you notice the ***sequence*** in these measures?

The B section ends with a ***perfect cadence*** in F major (mm. 35-36). In m. 36, Telemann adds an E flat to turn the F major chord into a ***dominant 7th*** of B flat major. This leads the music back to B flat major for the repeat of the A section.

The move to B flat minor in m. 55 creates a darker atmosphere. The sequence in mm. 63-68 moves through several keys. In m. 68, Telemann once again uses the G minor chord as a pivot to return to B flat major.

MINUET IN A MAJOR

List A: pp. 8-9

JOHN ALCOCK (1715-1806)

Alcock was trained as a chorister at St. Paul's Cathedral in his native London. After two positions as a parish church organist, he was appointed to Lichfield Cathedral in 1750. However, his fiery temperament led to disagreements with the church establishment. By 1765, his position as cathedral organist had come to an end. (Alcock published his side of the story in a semi-autobiographical novel, The Life of Miss Fanny Brown, *under a pseudonym in 1761.) He continued to live in Lichfield and served as organist in nearby parish churches until 1790. This minuet is from a set of six suites of dance movements published with a trumpet piece in London in 1741.*

Articulation

Play this *Minuet* with a light touch and smooth, flowing ***ornaments***. Experiment with ***articulation*** to find which touches will sound best in a particular passage.

For example, you might play the R.H. part of mm. 5-10 detached. Alternatively, try a combination of detached notes and slurs.

Ornaments

- The melody includes ***trills*** and ***mordents***. Practise each one separately, then incorporate it into the melody.
- Play the trills clearly and evenly. Don't accent the first note. When you practise them, set the metronome at ♪ = 72. Play steady eighth notes in the L.H.

This will help you to play the five notes of the trill evenly. When you play the L.H. as written, remember this eighth-note pulse.

The Left Hand

The L.H. provides a rhythmic anchor for the R.H. melody. Enhance the rise and fall of the L.H. line with subtle dynamic shading to support the R.H. phrase structure.

- Make the L.H. quarter notes slightly detached, but avoid a sharp or dry sound.
- Keep your hand close to the keyboard and use small finger movements. Try not to move your hand or arm too much.

PRACTICE TIP: In mm. 1-2, lift your L.H. after each note. This will enhance the articulation of the R.H. slurs. Play m. 2 (an ***imitation*** at a lower pitch) a little softer than m. 1.

Dynamics

Use terraced dynamics for the ***sequence*** in mm. 31-34. Shift up one level for each repetition. Start m. 31 *piano*, play m. 32 *mezzo piano*, m. 33 *mezzo forte*, and m. 34 *forte*.

Form

This *Minuet* is in ***binary form:***

A mm. 1-11
B mm. 12-39

In both sections, the main theme (mm. 1-4, 12-15, and 16-19) alternates with passages of steady eighth notes. These eighth-note passages develop ***motives*** from the main theme. They move the music through a variety of keys, often in a sequence pattern.

Modulations

- In the A section, the theme is stated in A major (mm. 1-4). The D sharp in m. 5 signals the ***modulation*** to E major, the ***dominant*** key.
- The B section opens with the main theme in E major. The theme is repeated in the home key of A major.
- In m. 20, the music shifts to F sharp minor. Alcock uses the melodic minor scale in the sequence pattern of mm. 21-23. The sixth and seventh degrees of the scale (D and E) are sharpened going up the scale in m. 20, but not coming down in m. 21. There is a ***perfect cadence*** (V-I) in F sharp minor in mm. 25-26.
- Alcock uses another sequence in mm. 27-30 to move through B minor to A major.
- The piece ends with one more sequence (mm. 31-34) and a cadence in the home key of A major.

ANDANTE IN E MINOR

List A: pp. 10-11

JOSEPH-HECTOR FIOCCO (1703-1741)

Fiocco was the son of an Italian composer and opera impresario who settled in Brussels. Joseph-Hector studied music with his father and an older brother. He became a professional musician in the royal chapel in Brussels and later at Antwerp Cathedral. In addition to his talents as an organist and harpsichordist, Fiocco was also a violin maker and a professor of Greek and Latin. Fiocco's only known harpsichord works are two suites of 12 movements each, published in Brussels in 1730. This Andante *is from the first suite.*

Balance

Imagine the lilting melody played by an oboe, and the sustained, *portato* accompaniment played by a string trio. Maintain a sensitive balance of sound between your hands. Keep the L.H. accompaniment softer than the melody, but bring out the moving L.H. lines in mm. 3, 6-12, 23-24, and 30-35. These notes change the ***harmonies***.

Rhythm

The *cantabile* melody and the steady L.H. eighth notes give this piece a constant rhythmic flow. The rhythms look simple but they can be tricky. Practise shifting in and out of the triplet rhythms. Count in eighth notes.

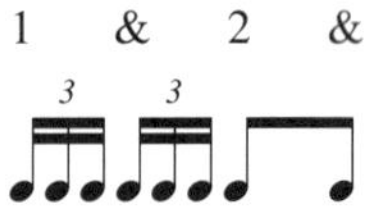

Be careful not to accent the sixteenth note after the tied note.

Ornaments

The ***ornaments*** help to move the music forward.

- Practise each ornament separately, then fit it smoothly into the melody.
- Start the ornaments on the beat and make a tiny *diminuendo*. Keep the notes light and don't accent the last note.

Phrasing

Establish where each phrase begins and ends. This will help you to understand the structure and direction of the music.

- The first phrase (mm. 1-4) is followed by two shorter phrases (mm. 5-6 and 7-8). Mark a little comma after the high A in m. 6 and the high G in m. 8. When you play, make a little break at the commas to allow the music to breathe.
- The long phrase in mm. 9-13 moves forward to the ***cadence*** in G major.

Dynamics

Once you have decided where the phrases begin and end, you can begin to shape them.

- In mm. 1-3, shape the dynamic levels to match the rise and fall of the melody.
- The longer phrase in mm. 14-23 rises gradually. The changing harmonies create musical tension. *Crescendo* (as marked) to the high point in m. 18. Give the notes in this measure a little extra time and weight. Then relax the intensity through mm. 19-23.

Sequences and Modulations

This music is mostly in the keys of E minor and G major. Fiocco uses ***sequences*** to change keys.

- For example, in mm. 5-8, the music moves through A minor (in mm. 5-6) to G major. The A minor ***tonic*** (I) chord in m. 6 is also the ***supertonic*** (II) chord of G major.
- In mm. 14-17, Fiocco uses a sequence to touch briefly on the keys of A major and B major. Then he uses the B major tonic chord (I) as a ***pivot***. This chord is the ***dominant*** (V) chord of the home key, E minor.

Plan the dynamics for each sequential passage and use terraced dynamics to highlight the repetitions.

GAVOTTA

List A: pp. 12-13

DOMENICO ZIPOLI (1688-1726)

Zipoli was trained under Alessandro Scarlatti in Naples and Bernardo Pasquini in Rome. In 1715 he was appointed organist of the Jesuit church in Rome. Zipoli joined the Jesuit order in 1716, and the next year he set sail from Seville to begin life as a missionary in Argentina. He was organist at the Jesuit church in Córdoba. In Argentina, he completed a course of study to become a priest, but he died of tuberculosis before he could be ordained. Zipoli's Sonate d'Intavolatura, *from which this* Gavotta *is taken, was published in Rome in 1716. This collection is in two parts. The first is for organ and the second for harpsichord. Zipoli's other compositions include two oratorios which were performed at the Jesuit church in Rome.*

A Three-Voice Texture

For the most part, this piece has a three-voice texture. The R.H. plays one voice, and the L.H. plays two voices. However, all three voices are not equal.

The upper voice has the melody. Let this voice sing out above the two lower voices with a good, round tone. Shape it expressively and pay close attention to the ***articulation***.

A Fourth Voice

- Zipoli adds extra voices to fill out the last chord of the ***cadences*** in mm. 14 and 31.
- In mm. 4-6, Zipoli adds a second voice to the R.H. This strengthens the R.H. sound. In these measures, you can play both hands with equal sound.
- A second R.H. voice is also implied in mm. 8-9.

Two Left-Hand Voices

The two lower voices provide ***harmony*** for the melody. However, don't dismiss the L.H. part as "accompanying chords." These two voices have melodic lines of their own. See, for example, the L.H. of mm. 8-9.

Your L.H. needs the same independence and control as your R.H. Shape the phrases with dynamics, and give each voice a singing, *legato* line. Study these voices closely so that you will be aware of their function in the three-part structure.

1. Play the upper L.H. voice with your R.H. and the lower L.H. voice with your L.H. Listen to the ***counterpoint***.
2. Play both voices with your L.H. Can you still hear the individual line of each voice?
3. Play each L.H. voice alone with the R.H. melody. Listen to the relationship between the two voices.
4. Play the music as written. Balance the sound so that each voice can be heard distinctly.

Articulation

This spirited *Gavotta* has a light, transparent sound.

- Use an even, controlled touch.
- Project each note clearly. (If necessary, write additional fingering in your music.)
- Balance the sound between your hands so that each voice can be heard.
- Try a combination of slurs and *staccatos* for the running eighth notes in the R.H.
- Play most L.H. notes detached. Hold quarter and half notes for their full value. (Give special attention to mm. 8-9 and 22.)

Dynamics and Phrasing

A musical phrase is an idea that has a beginning, a middle and an end.

- Think in long phrases. Build the sound up to a climax, then release the tension (with a *diminuendo*) as the phrase concludes.
- For example, in mm. 8-14, make a *crescendo* and *diminuendo* to match the rise and fall of the melody.
- Highlight the opening of each phrase. In this piece the phrases overlap. As one phrase ends, another begins. Here is a list of the phrases and cadences:

mm. 1-4	cadence in F major
mm. 4-8	cadence in F major
mm. 8-14	cadence in A minor
mm. 15-23	cadence in B flat major
mm. 23-31	cadence in D minor

Form

This work is in ***binary form***:

A	mm. 1-14
B	mm. 15-31

The main theme is stated at the beginning of each section (mm. 1-2 and 15-16). The rest of the piece consists of running eighth-note passages and ***sequences***.

Sequences

Sequences often have contrasting dynamics. In mm. 15-20, the first ***motive*** of the sequence is played *mezzo piano*, the second motive, *mezzo forte*, and the final motive, *forte*.

SONATA IN A MINOR
K 149, L 93

List A: pp. 14-15

DOMENICO SCARLATTI (1685-1757)

Domenico Scarlatti (the son of the opera composer Alessandro Scarlatti) was born in Naples. By age 16, Domenico had been appointed organist and composer at the royal chapel in Naples. He travelled throughout Italy and held posts in Venice and Rome. Sometime after 1719, Scarlatti became head of music at the royal court of Portugal in Lisbon and gave keyboard lessons to Maria Barbara, daughter of King John V. When Maria Barbara married the heir to the Spanish throne in 1729, Scarlatti moved to Spain with her court, and he spent the rest of his life there. His 555 well-known keyboard sonatas were written for the gifted Maria Barbara. Scarlatti was also a virtuoso performer, and has been called the founder of modern keyboard technique. The agile figures in his sonatas are proof of this.

Metre

This sonata is written in a minor key, but it has a bright, energetic character. The phrases begin on the upbeat. This gives a rhythmic "lift" to the music. Stress the first beat of the measure and keep the remaining beats lighter (especially the second and fourth).

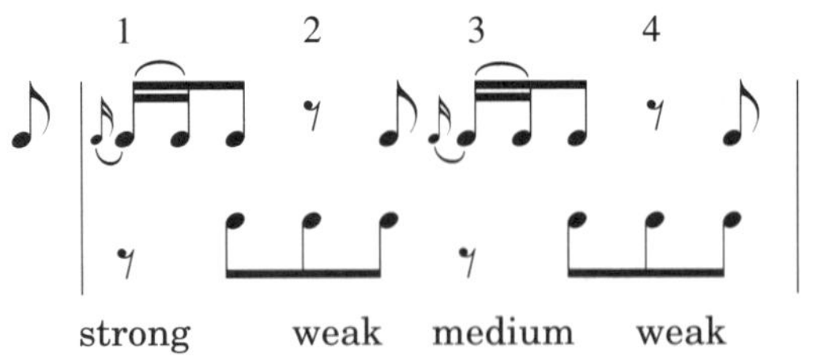

Musical Fingering

Good fingering can make a passage easier to play. Fingering also has a musical purpose. For example, in m. 1, if you use your fourth finger on the second beat, you can feel the division of the sixteenths into two groups of four.

- Change fingers on the long stretches of repeated notes. This alters the balance of your hand, giving a more rhythmic, varied tone.
- Find fingerings that allow your hand to shift positions in a way that makes musical sense.

Articulation

- Play most of the eighth notes detached.
- Make the sixteenth notes bright and clear. Let your arm float along with your hand as you play. Hold your hand a little higher over the black keys for good balance and control.
- Use a combination of slurred and *staccato* notes to give the music more colour and variety. (Imagine a violinist playing long bow strokes, and then bouncing the bow off the strings.)

Ornaments

- ***Ornaments*** are colourful additions. Play them with clarity, poise and control. Keep the notes even and blend them smoothly into the melody.
- Start the short ***trills*** on the note above the main note. Play them on the beat.
- The ***appoggiaturas*** in mm. 3 and 17-18 take half the value of the following note.

Form

This sonata has two sections:

A mm. 1-16
B mm. 17-31

- The opening ***motive*** is not repeated. Its function is to establish the mood and character of the piece. However, the second halves of the A and B sections are very similar.
- As in many of Scarlatti's sonatas, ideas are repeated for emphasis (see mm. 6-8 and 12).

Harmonic and Melodic Skeletons

The A section moves through the keys of A minor, C major, D minor, and E minor. The ***harmony*** is based on ***cadences***, that is, chords moving between the ***dominant*** and the ***tonic*** of each key.

- Look for the chords on which the melody is built. Play the circled notes as solid chords and listen to the harmony.

- Now look at the melody more closely. What do the circled notes in this example form?

- Play the music as written. Use the chords and scale patterns as a guide to help you to determine the direction of the music.

SARABANDE EN RONDEAU

List A: pp. 16

JOHANN SEBASTIAN BACH (1685-1750)

Among Bach's voluminous keyboard works are numerous suites in which the dances and national styles that were popular in the Baroque era are represented. The best-known works are the English Suites (BWV 806-811) *and the* French Suites (BWV 812-817). *There are six works in each set. In addition to these two collections, Bach also wrote individual keyboard suites. This* Sarabande *is the middle movement from a suite in F minor. It is preceded by a prelude and followed by a* gigue. *(The F minor suite is preserved only in a manuscript copy made by Johann Peter Kellner. Some scholars have doubted the work's authenticity.)*

Three Voices

There are three voices in this *Sarabande.* The L.H. plays two voices. (In mm. 14 and 26, Bach adds a third L.H. voice.) The L.H. voices are more than an accompaniment to the R.H. melody. There is often an independent L.H. line.

1. Play the R.H. melody all the way through.
2. Play the lower L.H. part.
3. Play the two L.H. voices together.

- When you play hands together, try to hear each voice independently. Be aware of the melodic movement in the upper L.H. voice.
- Balance the sound between this voice and the R.H. melody like a dialogue. Let each voice speak out in turn.
- Listen to the lowest voice. Let the R.H. melody sing out, but play the lowest voice so that it can be heard clearly.

Articulation

- This music is marked *cantabile*. Play each voice with a rich, singing tone.
- Project the R.H. melody by shifting arm weight to the fleshy pads of your fingers. For ease of movement, keep your arm relaxed and flexible.
- Play each voice *legato*. Overlap each note into the next and avoid sudden accents.
- Hold the longer notes for their correct value. These held notes sustain the ***harmony***.
- In the L.H., m. 16, hold the F and play the following C and F *portato* to emphasize the ***cadence***.

Phrasing and Dynamics

Shape the phrases in all three voices expressively. In speech, you use punctuation and the inflection of your voice to organize your thoughts into sentences. You can approach musical phrasing the same way.

- For example, the melodies in mm. 1-2 and 3-4 make up one phrase. The next long phrase is mm. 5-8. Make a slight break between each musical idea (for example, after the dotted half note in the R.H., m. 2), but keep the longer phrase structure in mind.
- In mm. 1-5, the R.H. melody rises from a low F to a high A flat. Enhance this shape with a gradual *crescendo* through mm. 3-5. Move the music toward the climax and taper the sound at the end.
- Remember to shape the L.H. voices. For example, in m. 2, give the upper L.H. voice a small *crescendo* to the C on the third beat, then *diminuendo* to the A in m. 3.

Form

This piece is in ***ternary form:***

A mm. 1-16
B mm. 17-28
A mm. 1-16

In spite of the fact that this piece has a key signature of three flats, the home key is F minor.

- In the A section, the main theme is played twice. What does Bach change in the repetition?
- The B section opens with a ***variation*** of the main theme, played in D flat major. This theme moves through different keys in a ***sequence*** pattern (mm. 21-24) with an echo effect (*mezzo forte, mezzo piano*). The section ends with a ***perfect cadence*** in C minor.

SONATA IN D MAJOR

List B: pp. 17-19

MATEO ALBÉNIZ (*ca* 1755-1831)

The influence of Domenico Scarlatti (1685-1757) in the Iberian peninsula extended over the next few generations of Spanish musicians. Scarlatti's keyboard sonatas served as a model for his pupil Antonio Soler (1729-1783). Mateo Albéniz, in turn, learned from the example of Soler. Albéniz earned his living mainly as a church musician. His sacred compositions were popular in northern Spain during his lifetime. He also helped introduce the music of Haydn and Mozart into Spain.

This sonata may remind you of Scarlatti's style. Look through the music to find these features:

- a fast, energetic character
- extensive use of octaves and repeated notes
- phrases in parallel 3rds
- broken-triad figures

A Flamenco Flavour

This sonata has a definite Spanish atmosphere. How does Albéniz transfer a guitar sound to the keyboard?

- Imagine playing mm. 1-8 on a guitar. You would play the L.H. notes with your thumb, and pick out the R.H. broken chords with your fingers.
- The repeated chords in mm. 23-24, 32-33, 35-36, 54-55, and 71-72 suggest rapid strumming. Albéniz uses these Flamenco-style chords as punctuation. They provide an exciting contrast to the gentler melodies. (Notice that most of these passages have *crescendos.*)
- Imagine a flamenco guitarist playing these chords while the dancers stamp their feet and clap their hands.

Motion and Metre

This sonata has an energetic rhythm.

- The melodies begin on an upbeat, which pushes the phrase over the bar line into the next measure.
- Stress only the first beat of each measure.
- For a still lighter effect, stress only the first beat of each short phrase. (For example, in mm. 1-7, stress the first beats of mm. 1 and 4.)

HINT: Count all the rests carefully. Lift your hand exactly on the beat. A release which is either too early or too late will weaken the rhythm.

Dynamics

- There is a lot of repetition in this piece. To broaden the scope of the music, use echo effects to suggest closeness and distance.
- Use changes of dynamic level to highlight the beginning of a new phrase or section. These contrasts will help you to clarify the structure for the listener.

Articulation

To improve your precision, practise at a medium tempo with a firm, *staccato* touch. Keep your wrist and arm relaxed and flexible. Give each note a bright, clear attack. When you have learned the notes, play the piece at a faster tempo with a slightly detached touch.

- Keep the L.H. repeated notes even. Change fingers on each note (3-2-1-3-2-1)
- Play the parallel 3rds, 10ths, and octaves exactly together.

PRACTICE TIP: Relax your hand during the dotted quarter notes preceding the ***grace notes*** in mm. 28 and 50. This will help you to control the ***ornaments*** and fit them lightly into the melody.

Form and Related Melodies

The two large repeated sections of this piece fall into a rather loose ***rounded binary form:***

A	*a*	mm. 1-15
	b	mm. 16-24
	a_1	mm. 25-36
	c	mm. 37-46
B	a_2	mm. 47-55
	a_3	mm. 56-72
A_1	*c*	mm. 73-84
	a	mm. 85-92

The contrasting B section has a more pronounced Spanish character. The R.H. phrases are more curved. Also the L.H. plays a more melodic line. Project it a little. The section begins with a ***variation*** of the "*a*" melody. This is followed by a faster, more energetic *tarantella*-like tune which combines references to the theme in mm. 25-36.

SONATINA IN F MAJOR
(FIRST MOVEMENT)

List B: page 20-21

WOLFGANG AMADEUS MOZART (1756-1791)

During Mozart's lifetime, the piano replaced the harpsichord as the favourite keyboard instrument. The instrument that Mozart had in his workroom was different from the piano of today. It had a smaller compass, a light and rapid action, and a bright sound. Mozart wrote 18 sonatas, 16 sets of variations, and a number of other pieces for the piano. However, this movement was not originally written for the piano. This music comes from Mozart's Five Divertimenti *for two clarinets and bassoon, K439b. He rearranged and transposed movements from the Divertimenti into the six* Viennese Sonatinas.

Playing a Trio

It is easy to find the three voices in this "trio."

- Sometimes the third voice is played by the L.H. (as in mm. 1-4).
- Sometimes the third voice is played by the R.H. (as in mm. 6-8).
- Sometimes the third voice is only suggested (as in the ***Alberti bass*** figure in mm. 4-5).

Practise different combinations of two voices and listen for the different patterns between the voices. Always be aware of the middle voice. Bring it out, but keep it softer than the upper, melody voice.

Playing Legato Lines

- Let the music flow seamlessly. Overlap each note into the next. Balance the weight of your arm on each finger in turn.
- When you play repeated notes (for example, in the L.H., m. 9), hold each note as long as possible before lifting to play the next one.
- Sometimes you change fingers on repeated notes. This varies the stress and helps you to shape the musical line.
- In m. 4, the L.H. plays the pattern from m. 1 at double speed. Keep this figure in the background. Give it a sustained, *legato* sound.
- The soaring, lyrical melody in mm. 14-15 is accompanied by broken sixteenth-note chords. Play the leaps and slurred figures with a flexible wrist. Keep the L.H. accompaniment controlled and even.

Playing 3rds and 6ths

Keep the R.H. 3rds and 6ths as *legato* as possible. Give the upper melody notes a stronger sound. To practise the R.H., mm. 6-8:

1. Play the upper line with the correct fingering. Join the notes smoothly together. Keep your arm and wrist relaxed.
2. Add the lower line, but just touch the keys with your thumb or second finger.
3. Play both lines together. Keep the upper line *legato* and play the lower line with a gently detached touch.
4. Play the R.H. part as written. Keep both voices as *legato* as possible. Gently detach the repeated thumb notes in the lower line.

Phrasing and Punctuation

A musical idea is like a sentence – it needs punctuation. Draw a small box (in pencil) at the end of each phrase.

- Write a punctuation mark (such as a period, a comma, or a colon) in each box.
- Now play the music. Time your pauses according to the punctuation: make a definite break for a period and a short lift for a comma.
- Listen as you play. Does your punctuation work?

Form

This movement is in ***rounded binary form*** with a *coda:*

A	mm. 1-8
B	mm. 8-16
A	mm. 16-24
coda	mm. 24-28

- In the A section, the theme is introduced and repeated with ***variations***.
- The B section ***modulates*** to C major, the ***dominant*** key. The R.H. plays variations on the theme. (Did you notice that the melody in 3rds from mm. 9-10 is ***inverted*** into 6ths in mm. 11-12?)

SCHERZO IN A MAJOR

List B: pp. 22-23

JOHANN NEPOMUK HUMMEL (1778-1837)

Hummel was born in Pressburg (Bratislava). He studied with Mozart and Haydn in Vienna, and toured widely as a child prodigy. In 1804, he became director of music for the Esterházy family of Hungary, taking over Haydn's duties while the elder musician retained the title of Kapellmeister. In 1811, Hummel returned to Vienna and resumed life as a touring virtuoso. He appeared in most major cities between London and St. Petersburg. He also held court appointments in Stuttgart (1816-1818) and Weimar (1819-1837).

The Main Theme

- The opening ***motive*** has a slur and a *staccato* note. Drop gently into the slur, and detach it from the *staccato* eighth note.
- The notes of the main theme (mm. 1-4) form an A major scale, beginning on the ***mediant*** (C sharp) and ending on the ***dominant*** (E). The L.H. thumb plays the last four notes (E, F sharp, G sharp, A).
- When the main theme is repeated in mm. 17-20, the L.H. plays an A melodic minor scale, beginning on the dominant (E).
- The main theme returns in m. 45. In mm. 53-56, the R.H. plays a sixteenth-note figure. Compare mm. 17-20 and 53-56.

- The L.H. repeats the main theme in mm. 53-56, with an A major scale.

Playing Scale Passages

- Play the scales with curved fingers.
- Aim for a brilliant, clear sound.
- Use the *crescendos* and *diminuendos* to shape the phrases.

To prepare for the scale passage in mm. 57-58, practise the A major scale in 10ths. Start with your R.H. third finger on C sharp and your L.H. fifth finger on A. Use the regular fingering.

The Left Hand

The 3/8 metre and the L.H. rhythm give this *Scherzo* a lilting, dance-like character. Imagine skating to this music.

- Play the L.H. of mm. 1-4. Feel a strong pulse on the first beat of each measure. Use a sweeping hand movement: drop into the low A and roll forward to the chord on the third beat, joining the notes gently. (Think of an energetic push and a graceful follow-through, like a slow, skipping step.)

Pedal Notes

- The L.H. plays E, the dominant, all the way through mm. 25-33. A prolonged bass note is called a ***pedal***. This E is a dominant pedal.
- The ***harmony*** above this pedal forms a series of dominant-***tonic*** (V-I) chords.

- In mm. 60-72, there is a tonic pedal. Can you find other places where Hummel uses a pedal note?

Listen for Voices

- In mm. 21-23, the L.H. plays two voices. Can you hear the duet?
- In mm. 60-72, the harmony is defined by the upper L.H. part, not the bass pedal.

Play the circled L.H. notes with the R.H. melody. Now add the other L.H. notes. Can you hear all three voices?

- Look for other three-voice sections. Play different two-voice combinations, then play all three parts together. Give each voice a good *legato* line.

RONDO IN G MAJOR
OP. 18, NO. 1

List B: pp. 24-27

JAN VÁCLAV VOŘÍŠEK (1791-1825)

Voříšek was born in Vamberk, in north-eastern Bohemia. He moved to Prague in 1806, then emigrated to Vienna in 1813. In Vienna he studied with Hummel, and when Hummel left Vienna in 1816, Voříšek took over his pupils. He became the conductor of the Gesellschaft der Musikfreunde in 1818, and in 1823 he was named court organist. He died of tuberculosis in 1825 at age 34. Voříšek's most important contribution was in the area of piano music. His expressive style is a link between the age of Beethoven and Schubert and the later Romantic piano music of Chopin and Smetana.

Form

In a ***rondo***, one theme is repeated between contrasting sections:

A mm. 1-18
B mm. 19-35
A_1 mm. 36-53
C mm. 54-72
A_2 mm. 73-104

Two Motives

There are two ***motives***. These motives and their ***variations*** dominate the entire work.

- The "*a*" motive (mm. 1-4) skips up a G major ***tonic*** chord, then floats down smoothly. The upbeat slurs propel the rhythm along. In the A_1 section, the "*a*" motive is ***ornamented*** with ***appoggiaturas*** (mm. 41 and 43).
- The energetic "*b*" motive (mm. 9-10) also begins on the upbeat. Keep the upbeat notes light, and *crescendo* over the bar line into the following measure. Change fingers on the repeated notes for a clearer ***articulation***.

PRACTICE TIP: Don't bump the note after the tie (for example, in mm. 2, 6, 12, and 13). Instead, match the dynamic level with the sound of the preceding note.

Section A_2

Section A_2 has a similar beginning to that of Section A, but there are surprises in store.

- Make a special event of the sudden key change in m. 84.
- In mm. 93-94, Voříšek jumps back and forth between G major and G minor. When G major wins, play it triumphantly. Follow with a smooth *diminuendo* as the music tiptoes *pianissimo* into the high register.
- The final surprise is the strong, decisive ending. Play the ***trill*** lightly and keep your fingers close to the keys. Cut back the dynamic level so you can also highlight the two final chords.

Section B

- In the B section, an inversion of the "*a*" motive is used in a ***sequence*** (mm. 19-26).
- Then the music shifts abruptly to E flat major. Here Voříšek decorates the "*a*" motive with sixteenth notes. In mm. 29 and 31-32, accent the "strong" R.H. sixteenth notes.

- The B section ends on a D major chord (the ***dominant*** of G major). This leads directly back to A_1.

Section C

- The more dramatic section C is in G minor, the tonic minor. The chordal texture, shorter phrases, lower register, and dynamic changes all provide a strong contrast.
- A new motive – a slurred jumping figure – appears in one hand and is ***imitated*** by the other (mm. 54, 58, 62, 66). This figure is extended as the music passes through C minor and returns to G minor. Vary the intensity of the *fortes* in mm. 62 and 66 with the changes of key.
- In m. 67, the slurs in both hands suddenly change direction. The section ends, again on a D major chord.

Left-Hand Accompaniment

- The upward direction of the broken-triad accompaniment enhances the cheerful mood.
- Practise the L.H. in solid chords. This will help you to become familiar with the ***harmony***.
- Keep the L.H. accompaniment light and soft. Direct more energy and arm weight toward the R.H.

These exercises will help you to make the eighth-note figures even and smooth:

1. Play the L.H. part *staccato*. Balance your hand above the centre of each note. Keep your wrist and arm relaxed.
2. Accent the first note of each three-note group. Repeat, accenting the second, then the third notes.
3. Play the L.H. part in different rhythms.

CHILDREN'S SONATA OP. 118A, NO. 1
(SECOND MOVEMENT: THEME AND VARIATIONS)

List B: pp. 28-29

ROBERT SCHUMANN (1810-1856)

Schumann was one of the central figures of the Romantic movement in music, both as a composer and as a perceptive and influential music critic. Schumann's early works were for piano. In 1840, inspired by his marriage to Clara Wieck, he wrote 150 songs. Later, he turned to orchestral, chamber, and choral music. Mental problems plagued Schumann for much of his life. When he was happy, he wrote quickly. At other times, plunged into despair, he was unable to compose. After an attempted suicide in 1854, he was confined to an insane asylum. Schumann's Children's Sonatas, *Op. 118 were written in June 1853. The three sonatas were dedicated to Schumann's three eldest daughters, Julie, Elise and Marie.*

Form

The theme is stated in mm. 1-6. Schumann presents five ***variations*** on this theme, and the movement ends with a short *coda*.

- Can you find the theme in each variation? Draw circles around the melody notes.
- Each variation has the same chord progression but the arrangement of notes may vary. Look for these triads:

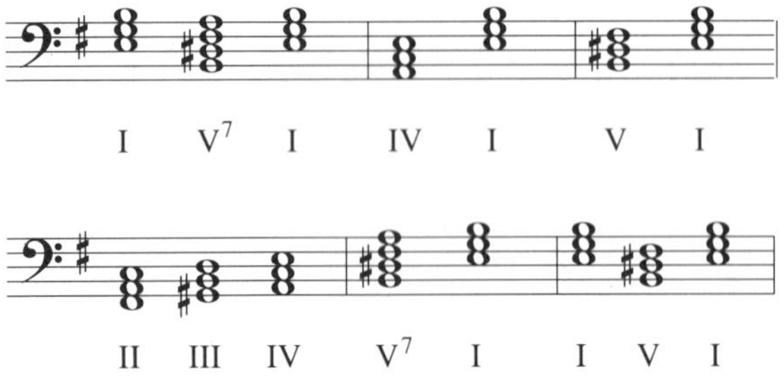

The Theme

- Think of the theme as one long phrase. Use the upbeats in each measure to push the music forward over the bar line.

- The falling 3rds have a sad, wistful quality. Avoid the temptation to make a *diminuendo* with this figure.
- Don't let the sixteenth rests disrupt the melody. Use a gentle touch. (Think of steps in deep snow.) Add a touch of pedal on each chord to enrich the sound.
- Follow the dynamics. The theme begins *mezzo forte* and increases to *forte* as the melody rises. The "question" in mm. 1-4 is answered *piano* in mm. 5-6.

Melody and Counterpoint

- This movement has a three- or four-voice texture. Be aware of each voice. Practise combinations of two voices (for example, "soprano" and "tenor" or "alto" and "bass"). When you play the music as written, listen for the ***counterpoint*** between the voices.
- Bring out whichever voice has the theme. Give the theme a *cantabile* tone, and use a little more arm weight for the melody notes.

The Variations

- Variation 1 (mm. 7-12) has an eighth-note accompaniment figure in the R.H.
- In Variation 2 (mm. 13-18), the L.H. plays the theme. The R.H. continues the eighth-note pattern with a counter-melody in the top notes.
- In Variation 3 (mm. 19-24), the R.H. plays the theme with a decorative triplet figure. Schumann also adds an upper L.H. voice. The ***syncopations*** created by the tied notes in mm. 19, 20, and 22 lend buoyancy.
- The shift to E major gives Variation 4 (mm. 25-30) a more energetic character. The theme is in the top voice of a four-part chordal texture. Bring out the dotted figure in the lower voices.
- In Variation 5 (mm. 31-36), the music returns to E minor. Schumann weaves the theme into a sixteenth-note pattern. Play the theme with a *tenuto* touch. Follow the slurs and *staccatos*. Plan the *ritardando* so that you don't slow down too soon.

Coda (mm. 37-40)

The *coda* continues the sixteenth-note activity and brings the music to a graceful close. Slow the music down a little (*un poco più lento*) and make the ***grace notes*** expressive.

SONATA IN G MAJOR
HOB. XVI/27 (SECOND MOVEMENT: MINUET)

List B: pp. 30-32

FRANZ JOSEPH HAYDN (1732-1809)

For nearly 30 years, Haydn worked at the country estate of the Esterházy family of Hungary, composing a wide variety of music and preparing musicians for weekly performances. He said himself that his isolation from the music centres of Europe forced him to become original. In his early sixties, Haydn embarked on two highly successful (and profitable) trips to London (1791-1792 and 1794-1795). After his return, he lived in Vienna. In 1802 he became ill, and he led a quiet life until his death in 1809. This Sonata in G Major *dates from 1776.*

This movement consists of a *Minuet* and a *Trio*. Both parts have a graceful rhythm. Keep a steady tempo through both parts. Feel a steady pulse of one strong beat for every two measures. This will help you to move the music along with a longer and lighter line.

MINUET

- The triplet rhythms in the melody have a charming, elegant character. They add lightness and move the music forward to the ***cadences***. Shape them with *crescendos* and *diminuendos*.
- Plan the ***articulation*** carefully, with attention to details such as the delicate slurs in mm. 4, 14, 16, and 18.
- Keep the ***ornaments*** smooth, and let each note sound clearly. Pay attention to your fingerwork, and avoid sudden hand movements.

Form

This section is in ***rounded binary form***:

A	mm. 1-14
B + A_1	mm. 15-24; 25-42

- The B section is similar to the A section. It opens with the same ***motive*** (this time ***transposed*** to D major), then quickly returns to G major.
- The A_1 section has the same material as the A section, but the repeated motives are different.

Humour

- The A section begins with a four-measure phrase. After m. 7, we expect the second four-measure phrase to conclude with a ***modulation*** to D major.
- Instead, the R.H. goes off on a joy ride! It "sticks" in one figure for four measures (like a broken record) before it finally breaks free to finish the phrase with a D major cadence in m. 14.
- In the A_1 section, Haydn delays the completion of a phrase by taking a figure through three octaves (mm. 29-31). In mm. 35-38, a second figure is repeated before the section finally glides to a close.
- Humour is a special quality in Haydn's music. Use variety and contrast to bring out the teasing character of these repetitions.

The Left Hand

- Play the L.H. softly and use a light, detached touch. Keep your fingers close to the keys.
- Keep the triplet figure smooth. Practise these passages by moving your fingers along the notes without pressing down the keys. Gradually add more weight until you reach the volume you need for a good balance of sound.

TRIO

The contrasting *Trio* has a quieter, more serious character. Play with a *cantabile* tone and a *legato* touch. Use subtle dynamics to shape the rise and fall of the shorter melodic figures.

Form

The *Trio* is also in rounded binary form:

A	mm. 43-50
B + A_1	mm. 51-58; 59-66

- The A section is in G minor. (This darker sound contrasts with the bright G major of the *Minuet*.)
- The contrasting B section is in B flat major. The repeated motive in mm. 51-54 builds to a climax in m. 55. Make each repetition a little louder than the one before.
- Think of the rests as windows that let in fresh air. Count carefully and lift for each one, but do not let these short silences break the musical line.

Technical Details

- Keep the slurs and decorative ornaments clear and elegant. Practise them separately at a slow tempo, then fit them smoothly into the melody.
- In mm. 43-46, make sure both notes of the L.H. 3rds sound together.
- Keep the L.H. octaves in mm. 51-54 light. Relax your wrist. (Tension in the wrist may cause a heavy or uneven sound.)

WALTZ IN B MINOR

List C: page 33

FRANZ SCHUBERT (1797-1828)

The son of a Viennese schoolmaster, Schubert received a first-class musical and general education, first at his father's school and later at the Imperial Choir School. He spent all his spare time making music. After a period as a teacher in his father's school, he quit in 1818 to devote himself entirely to composing music. In the remaining ten years of his life, music poured forth in great abundance – symphonies, operas, chamber music, piano works, church music, and over 600 songs. Schubert was never a financial success, but he was supported by a circle of friends who were always ready to help him get by. Schubert wrote over 300 short dances. This waltz comes from a set of 12 dances written between 1815 and 1821. They were intended for amateur musicians and are probably very much like the dances Schubert improvised for his friends at parties.

Left-Hand Accompaniment

Waltzes need a buoyant rhythm. The L.H. plays a typical waltz accompaniment – two chords bouncing up from a single bass note. Practise the L.H. separately.

- Feel a strong-weak-weak pulse.
- Stress the downbeat of each measure gently.
- Play the L.H. chords lightly. Wherever possible, play the bottom note of these chords with your fourth finger (instead of your fifth finger). This movement is easier and will give you better accuracy and a lighter tone.

Right-Hand Melody

- Let the melody sing out above the accompaniment. Listen carefully for a sensitive balance between the hands.
- In most measures, there is an accented note on the second beat. This slight ***syncopation*** contrasts with the waltz pulse in the L.H.

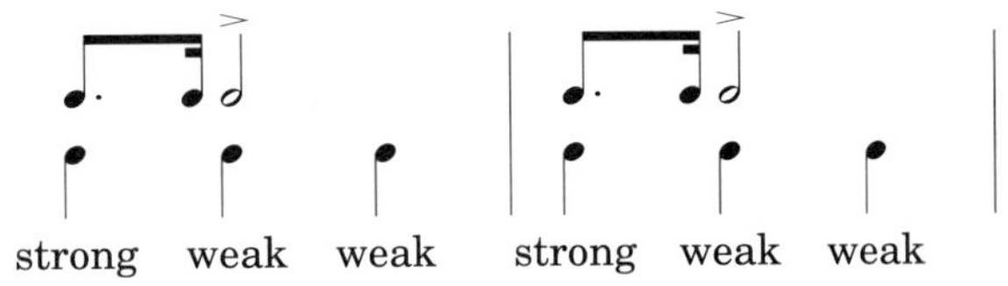

PRACTICE TIP: Project the top R.H. notes in mm. 31-32. Direct more energy into the fourth and fifth fingers to give this ending a bright tone.

Form

This waltz is in ***rounded binary form:***

A mm. 1-16
B + A_1 mm. 17-24; 25-32

The music is mostly in the key of B minor.

- There is a brief ***modulation*** to D major (the relative major) at the end of the A section.
- Section A_1 is a shortened version of section A ***transposed*** into B major (the ***tonic*** major).

Phrasing and Dynamic Shaping

- The music falls naturally into four-measure phrases. Make a slight break at the phrase endings to allow the music to breathe.
- Each phrase contains smaller slurred groups. Lift at the end of each slur, but keep the music moving toward the climax and the end of the longer phrase.
- The A and A_1 sections are marked *pianissimo.* Add subtle dynamic shaping within this quiet range to add interest and expression.

- The B section has a series of "question and answer" ***motives*** marked *mezzo forte* and *piano*. Emphasize these dynamic contrasts.

The Pedal

Use *legato* pedalling to give this music a smooth, full sound.

- Catch the bass note on the downbeat of each measure with the pedal and blend it into the next chord. The bass note and the chord are both part of the same ***harmony***.
- Change the pedal with the changes of harmony. Listen carefully to avoid blurring different chords together.

RONDINO

List C: pp. 34-35

TALIVALDIS KENINS (1919-)

Kenins was born in Latvia. He began playing the piano at age five and composing at age seven. He studied in France for a career in the diplomatic service (following in the footsteps of his father, who was a Latvian government official). After his return to Latvia, he studied music from 1940 to 1944 under Joseph Wihtol. After further studies at the Paris Conservatory (1945-1951), he moved to Canada. He taught at the University of Toronto from 1952 until his retirement in 1984.

Form

Rondino has a ***ternary form***. The sixteenth-note ***motive*** from the A theme keeps popping up all the way through. In a ***rondo form***, the A theme keeps coming "around," in between contrasting passages. This piece is not a fully-developed rondo. Here is the structure:

A	mm. 1-8
bridge	mm. 9-11
B	mm. 12-19
B_1	mm. 20-27
A_1	mm. 28-35
coda	mm. 36-40

- The A theme is in D major.
- The B theme is in G major (the ***subdominant*** key). The melody is in the L.H.
- In the B_1 section, the hands are reversed. The R.H. plays the melody an octave higher. Can you see any other differences? At the end, the music moves back to D major.
- The A_1 section has a different ending.
- The *coda* uses motives from the A theme and the bridge.

Melody and Accompaniment

- The melody of this energetic, light-spirited piece is played mostly by the R.H.
- In the A sections, the L.H. plays an accompaniment figure. Give more tone and weight to the melody. Listen carefully for a good balance of sound between the hands.
- In the B section, the R.H. plays a counter-melody. Play both hands with clear ***articulation*** and equal sound.

Articulation

- *Staccato* notes play an important role in both the melody and accompaniment. Make the *staccatos* short and use a light, crisp touch. Keep your fingers close to the keys.
- Give the accented notes a pointed, bright sound.
- Bring out the *marcato* passages in mm. 8, 26, and 34, but keep your arm relaxed. Avoid a hard, aggressive tone.
- Give the passages or notes marked ***rinforzando*** or ***sforzando*** a little more energy and dramatic emphasis, but avoid a strident tone. (Use touches of rhythmic pedalling to enhance the tone.)

Rhythm

Rondino has a dance-like character and a simple, lively rhythm. Gently stress the downbeat of each measure. The sixteenth-note figure from the rhythm of the A section dominates the piece.

Dynamics and Phrasing

- Kenins uses five levels of dynamics in this piece. Circle the dynamic markings in your music (in pencil). Can you see a pattern to the dynamics? What levels are used with each theme?
- Most of the phrases in this piece are four measures long. The *coda* (mm. 36-40) has two shorter phrases: mm. 36-38 and mm. 39-40. Always think forward to the end of each phrase to propel the music along.
- Shape each phrase carefully, and follow the *crescendos* and *diminuendos* in the music. Here is a suggestion for the first phrase:

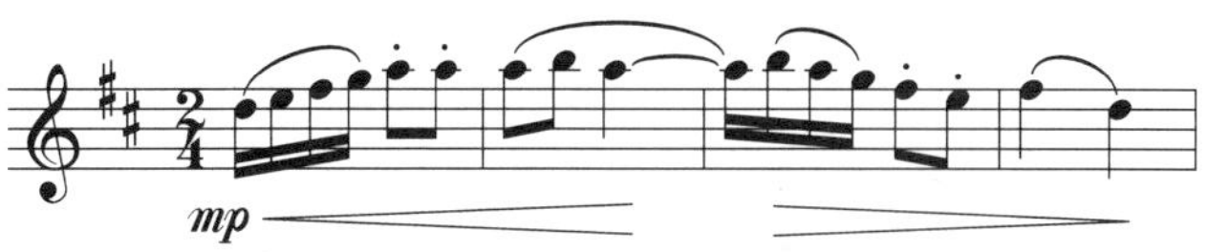

THE LITTLE ORPHAN GIRL
OP. 1, NO. 9

List C: page 36

ENRIQUE GRANADOS (1867-1916)

Granados was born in Lérida, Catalonia, in northeastern Spain. He studied piano and composition in Barcelona and in Paris. He returned to Barcelona in 1889. In 1901 he founded the Academia Granados, a centre for training pianists. As a composer, his biggest success was Goyescas *(1911), a piano suite based on paintings by Francisco José Goya y Lucientes. The Paris Opera encouraged Granados to write an opera based on the music, but the outbreak of World War I prevented a Paris production. The opera* Goyescas *was staged at the Metropolitan Opera in 1916, and Granados travelled to New York for the premiere. On the return trip to Europe, his ship was torpedoed by a German submarine. Granados was rescued, but he jumped back into the sea to try to save his wife. Tragically, both of them drowned.*

Melody

- The R.H. plays two voices. Pay close attention to the fingering. It will help you to play both voices *legato*. Focus more weight on the top notes of the R.H. part.
- Practise the R.H. melody alone (with the correct fingering). Imagine a violin or flute playing this plaintive tune.
- Use *legato* pedalling for a smooth, rich tone. Change the pedal with each change of ***harmony***. Listen carefully to avoid blurring the melody.
- The L.H. also plays melodic passages (for example, in mm. 4, 8, 10, and 12). Shape these little waves of melody expressively.

Rhythm

The rhythms have a Spanish flair.

1. The L.H. accompaniment repeats a ***syncopated*** rhythm, with a ***variation***.

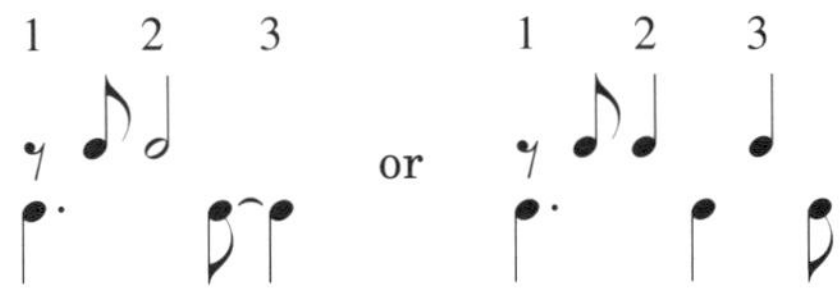

   The lower R.H. voice is part of the accompaniment and fits into this rhythm. Practise the L.H. separately, then add the lower R.H. voice (with the correct fingering).

2. The rhythm of the melody also has decorative variations.

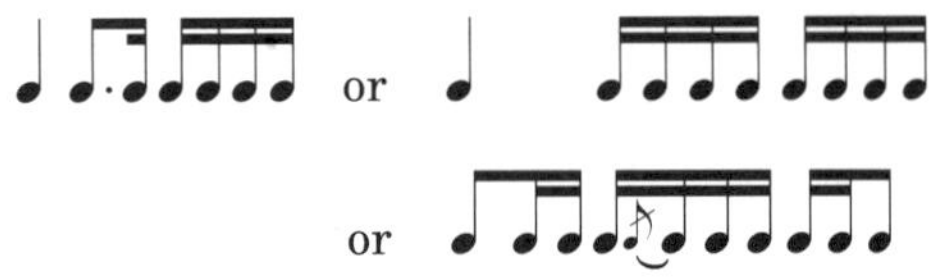

3. The rhythms of the L.H. "waves" (for example, mm. 4 and 8) are similar.

Practise tapping the two rhythms hands together. Count sixteenths so you can place the first R.H. sixteenth note correctly.

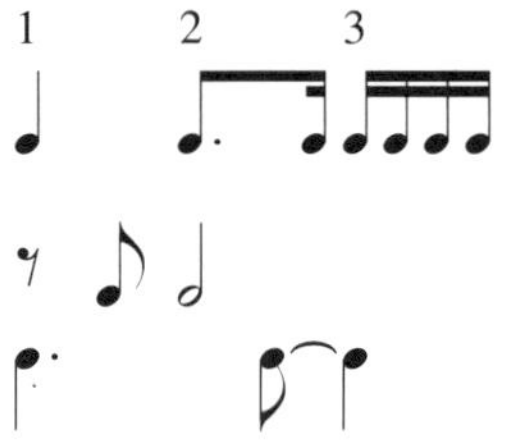

PRACTICE TIP: Give the accented notes in mm. 17 and 18 a gentle stress. Remember that the dynamic marking is *piano*.

Form

This piece has four sections:

A mm. 1-8
B mm. 9-16
A_1 mm. 17-20 with repeat
B_1 mm. 21-24

Phrasing

The melody falls into two- and four-measure phrases. Mark the phrase ends in your music.

- The phrases are made up of shorter slurred figures. Link the shorter slurs together into a single, long line.
- Make a tiny break at the end of the slurs and a slightly larger break at the end of each phrase to allow the music to breathe.

Harmony

- This piece is mostly in the key of B minor. However, the phrases in the B sections end on B major chords (mm. 12, 16, and 24).
- In sections A and A_1, the L.H. plays a repeated B (the ***tonic***). This continuous sound of one note is called a ***pedal***. (It gets its name from the long pedal notes played on an organ.) In the B section, the bass alternates between F sharp (the ***dominant***) and B.

WALTZ IN G SHARP MINOR
OP. 39, NO. 3

List C: page 37

JOHANNES BRAHMS (1833-1897)

As a child, Brahms learned the piano, violin, cello and horn. In his teens he was already composing and giving piano recitals. The year 1853 was a turning point in his life. In this year Brahms met his life-long friends Joseph Joachim, and Robert and Clara Schumann. Robert Schumann predicted that Brahms would be the next great composer. But Brahms was highly self-critical. He often discarded works that he felt were inferior, and he sent his new pieces to Joseph Joachim and Robert and Clara Schumann for their comments and criticisms.

Brahms eventually settled in Vienna, where he turned out one masterpiece after another. He was influenced by the popular music of Vienna, and was a close friend of the "waltz king," Johann Strauss the younger. The 16 Waltzes, *Op. 39 were written for piano duet in 1865. In 1867 Brahms arranged them for piano solo. Later he made a simplified version of the piano solo arrangement, and also adapted five of the waltzes for two pianos.*

Melody

The graceful melody of this waltz has wide leaps and is built on one rhythm. Project the melody over the L.H. accompaniment with a singing tone. Use arm weight to achieve a resonant, beautiful sound.

- Feel a gentle pulse of three beats per measure and stress the downbeat. Keep the first and third eighth notes light and give a subtle stress to the second eighth note.
- Try not to accent the top note of the leaps. Instead, use the three-eighth-note figure to lift the music forward to the next measure.

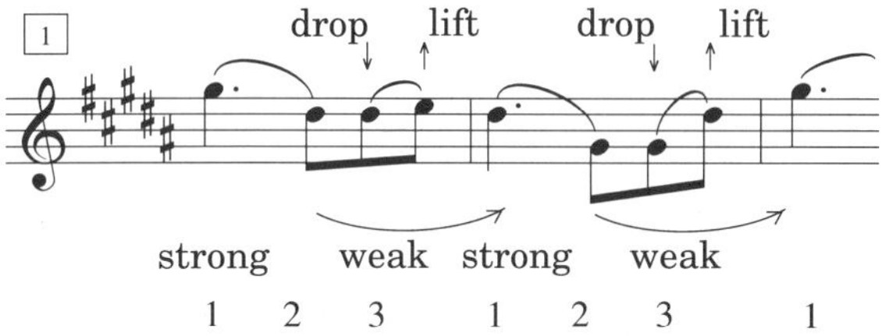

Accompaniment

The L.H. plays a typical waltz accompaniment.

- Feel a strong-weak-weak pulse. Stress the downbeat gently and make the chords light.
- Wherever possible, play the bottom note of these chords with your fourth finger (instead of your fifth finger). This will give you greater ease of arm movement, increased accuracy, and a lighter tone.
- Experiment with the L.H. fingering of the rest of the piece. When you find a fingering that fits your hand comfortably, write it in your music and use it every time you practise.
- Arpeggiate the L.H. chords with the wavy lines in mm. 9 and 11. Begin just before the beat. The top note of the chord should sound at the same time as the right-hand Ds. Use the pedal to blend the notes together.

Articulation and Dynamics

- This waltz has four-measure phrases. Make a small break at the phrase endings to allow the music to breathe.
- Lift slightly at the end of each R.H. slur, but keep the longer phrase in mind. Move the music toward the climax of each phrase and taper the phrase endings gracefully.
- Shape each phrase, matching the rise and fall of the melody with small *crescendos* and *decrescendos*. Brahms has marked some of these details in the music (for example, mm. 9-14). Always follow the composer's markings.

Rubato

A subtle ***rubato*** will help you to capture the Romantic style of this music. Use small *accelerandos* and *ritardandos* to add expression to the melody and enhance the dynamic shaping.

The Pedal

Use the pedal to help you keep the melody smooth and to enhance the tone. Co-ordinate your pedalling with the chord changes in the L.H. Listen carefully to the sound. Avoid blurring the melody.

Form

This piece is in ***binary form:***

A mm. 1-8
B mm. 9-16

MASTER MICHAEL

List C: page 38

WITOLD LUTOSŁAWSKI (1913-1994)

Lutosławski was born in Warsaw, and studied at the Warsaw Conservatory. Most of his early works were lost during World War II. After the war he worked briefly for Polish Radio, then devoted himself to composition. His first post-war works, including Folk Melodies *(1945, from which* Master Michael *is taken) and* Concerto for Orchestra *(1950-1954), were influenced by Bartók. Later, through meeting John Cage in 1961 and getting to know his music, Lutosławski developed his own version of chance music. He toured widely to lecture on and conduct performances of his music in Europe and North America.*

This expressive piece is an arrangement of a folk song from the Kurpia region of Poland.

Form

This piece is in ***binary form***:

Introduction	mm. 1-4
A	mm. 5-12
B	mm. 13-20
B_1	mm. 21-30
coda	mm. 31-38

- The B section is built on a ***sequence***.
- All three sections are repeated. The first ending of the B_1 section acts as a *codetta*, leading back to the A section.
- The second ending is a longer *coda*, built on the ***motive*** from the last two measures of the B section.

Melody

- The melody is in A minor. It moves mainly by step and stays mostly within a five-finger position. The music falls into four-measure phrases.
- Play this melody with a singing *legato* and well-shaped phrases.
- In mm. 17-20 and 25-28, the L.H. plays a counter-melody. Shape the *legato* phrases in both hands, but keep the L.H. a little quieter than the R.H.

Harmony

The L.H. jumps from one octave to another with sharply contrasting ***chromatic harmonies***.

- Study these chords and learn the patterns. This will help you to memorize the notes and play the L.H. part with a fluent rhythm.
- Be sensitive to the balance of sound. Don't let the more complex accompaniment overwhelm the simple melody.

In the A section, the 5ths on the first beat of each measure move through the circle of 5ths from A to F.

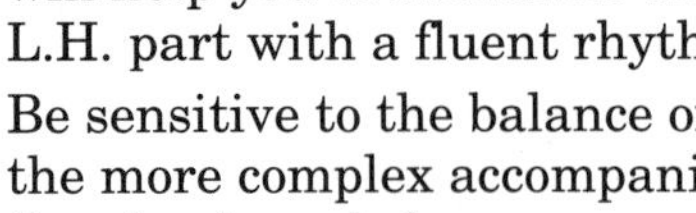

The chords on the second beat move down chromatically.

Now compare the L.H. part of the B and B_1 sections. The 6ths and 7ths of the B section are ***inverted*** into 3rds and 2nds in the B_1 section.

Metre and Tempo

This folk song is a waltz. Stress the first beat of each measure.

- The chords on the weaker second beats in the A section have a ***syncopated*** effect. Use this to create rhythmic interest.
- Use the changing tempos (for example, *poco ritardando*, *poco meno mosso*) to enhance the contrasting moods of this piece.
- There is a *ritardando* at the end of both B sections, but not at the end of the piece. Move the final measures along in a steady *allegro* tempo.

Articulation

- Give this music a warm, singing tone. Use a little rhythmic pedalling to add melodic flow and sonority.
- Lutosławski has written slurs on single quarter notes (for example, in m. 1). Lift off these notes slowly. Let the sound carry into the next beat. (You might hold the pedal down a little longer for these notes.)
- For the *poco forte* passage in mm. 13-20, keep your arms and wrists relaxed. Avoid a percussive touch.
- For a *pianissimo* in the beginning and ending, keep your fingers close to the keys. (You can use the soft pedal to help you control the *pianissimo*.)

PRELUDE IN E MINOR
OP. 28, NO. 4

List C: page 39

FRÉDÉRIC CHOPIN (1810-1849)

Chopin was born and educated in Warsaw, Poland. From an early age it was clear that his only real interest in life was music, and his only real interest in music was the piano. Most of Chopin's compositions are for piano solo. He settled in Paris in 1831. He seemed cut out for a career as a piano virtuoso, but after he moved to Paris he rarely appeared in public. Instead, he flourished in the atmosphere of that city's private salons. He made his living by publishing his music and giving lessons to well-to-do pupils. From 1838 to 1846, he lived with Aurore Dudevant, a French novelist who wrote under the name of George Sand. After this relationship ended, Chopin's already poor health declined rapidly. He died of tuberculosis at age 39.

Chopin's 24 Preludes, *Op. 28 (1836-1839) cover all 24 major and minor keys, in imitation of Bach's* Well-Tempered Clavier. *Most of the preludes are short and explore a single musical idea. The styles, textures and moods cover a wide range.* Prelude in E Minor *is one of the most lyrical.*

A Singing Tone

Project the melancholy R.H. melody over the L.H. chords. Play it with a singing tone.

- Direct the weight of your arm into your fingers. Keep your arm relaxed so you can move it easily. Shape each phrase carefully.
- Focus the weight on the top notes of the final three R.H. chords so they will sing out.

Dynamics and Dynamic Shaping

This piece begins *piano*. The next dynamic marking is the *forte* in m. 17. Let the sound grow gradually through these 17 measures.

- Follow the smaller *crescendos* and *decrescendos* in the music.
- Add tiny *crescendos* and *diminuendos* as the melody rises and falls. Shape the repeated figures.

- Increase the volume as the melody begins to move a little faster (for example, in mm. 9 and 12).

Left-Hand Accompaniment

- Play the L.H. chords quietly and smoothly. Keep your fingers in contact with the keys. Press the keys slowly down to the keybed. This will help you to avoid unwanted accents.
- Think of a rhythmic pulse of two beats per measure. Give each downbeat a subtle stress. This will help the music to flow.
- Co-ordinate your pedalling with the chord changes in the L.H. (Listen carefully. Don't blur the melody.) The pedal marks in mm. 17-18 are Chopin's own. Follow them exactly.

Rubato

- ***Rubato***, or rhythmic flexibility, is an essential part of Chopin's style. Use *rubato* with taste and discretion. Listen to the changes of ***harmony*** in the L.H. Use the points of harmonic tension and relaxation to guide your tempo changes.
- The climax of this prelude (mm. 16-18) is marked *stretto*. (*Stretto* is an Italian word meaning "drawn together.") Increase the tempo a little in these measures.

PRACTICE TIP: In m. 18, the R.H. plays a triplet against two eighth notes in the L.H. Fit the second L.H. eighth note between the second and third eighth notes of the R.H. triplet:

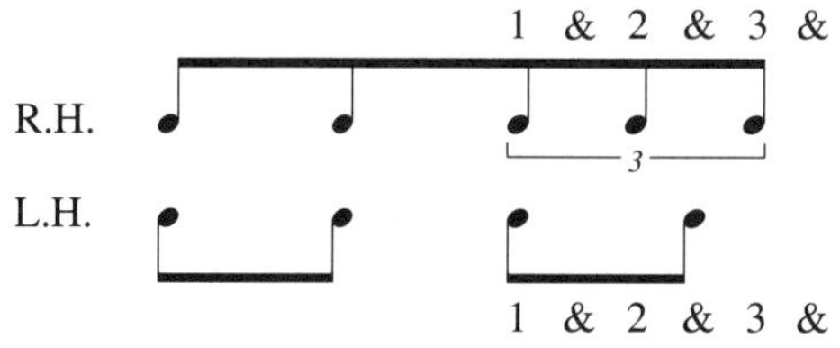

Ornaments

- Play the ***grace notes*** in mm. 11 and 19 quickly, just before the beat.
- Here are two suggestions for the ***turn*** in m. 16:

Form

This prelude has two sections:

A mm. 1-12
A_1 mm. 13-25

Both sections are in the key of E minor. The main theme is introduced in section A and repeated with ***variations*** in section A_1.

A JOKE

List C: pp. 40-41

PIERRE GALLANT (1950-)

Pierre Gallant was born in the Ottawa Valley. He moved to Toronto in 1970 to complete his ARCT at The Royal Conservatory of Music. He studied with Patricia Holt, Harry Freedman, and Samuel Dolin. In 1979, he joined the faculty of The Royal Conservatory of Music, where he teaches piano, theory, and composition. Gallant has written solo, chamber, and orchestral works, and music for the theatre. Since 1980, Gallant has also composed many pieces for The Royal Conservatory of Music piano and guitar repertoire albums. A Joke *was composed in 1970. It is one of a set of pieces called* Five Easy Pieces.

The teasing rhythms and crunchy ***dissonances*** give this zany little piece a definite 20th-century sound.

A Dynamic Joke?

Gallant uses surprise to make this piece into a joke. Did you notice the sudden changes of dynamics and register?

- The dynamic markings range from *pianissimo* to *fortissimo*, and the levels are constantly changing.
- Exaggerate these contrasts. (The *subito* in mm. 14 and 19 indicates a sudden change.)
- Follow the *crescendos* and *diminuendos* in the music. They will help you to shape the rather fragmented melody.

A Musical Laugh

The main ***motive*** is a musical representation of a laugh. Gallant uses it throughout the piece.

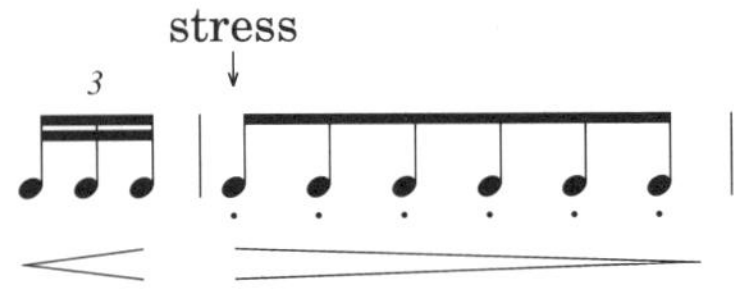

- Play the triplet smoothly. Make a tiny *crescendo* into the following eighth note.
- Give a slight stress to the first note of the eighth-note figure.
- In mm. 6-7, this motive crosses the bar line. Still stress the first eighth note. The shifted accent is part of the joke.

Articulation

- Most of the notes in this piece have an ***articulation*** mark of some kind. These too are part of the joke. Make a good contrast between the slurs and the *staccatos*.
- Use the *tenuto* notes for contrast as well. Hold these notes for their full value and give them a slight stress.
- The *staccato* notes and passages heighten the sense of fun. Give the *staccatos* a bright, crisp tone. Keep your fingers close to the keys.
- The *fortissimo* octaves in the R.H., mm. 19-22, are marked with accents. Let these octaves explode like the punch line of a joke. Play them with a firm touch and make them slightly detached.

PRACTICE TIP: Prepare for the octaves in mm. 20-22 so you can play them accurately.

1. Play the G octave and move your hand quickly down to the B octave. Land silently on the keys a fraction of a beat early.
2. When you can do this easily, play both octaves in the correct time.
3. Practise each position shift this way.

Form

The form of this work is free, but it falls into three sections.

- The first section (mm. 1-22) is based mainly on the "laugh motive."
- The middle section (mm. 23-30) is based in part on the R.H. figure from m. 15. Project the R.H. melody above the accompanying figure. This section is in 4/4. Keep a steady quarter-note beat as you change time signatures, and follow each *ritardando* and *a tempo*.
- The final section (mm. 31-38) is again based mostly on the "laugh motive." Play this final section with a gentle, teasing quality.

SONG AND ALBORADA
OP. 111, NO. 14

List C: pp. 42-43

JENÖ TAKÁCS (1902-)

Takács has lived and travelled in many different countries, and his music reflects this cosmopolitanism. He studied piano and composition in Vienna, and he has taught music in Egypt, the Philippines, Hungary and Switzerland. From 1952 to 1971, he taught piano at the University of Cincinnati. After retiring, he returned to his home town of Siegendorf in Austria. He has written orchestral, vocal and chamber works as well as many sets of piano pieces.

Song and Alborada *is from a set of 21 pieces titled* From Far Away Places. *The style and the mood change abruptly in this piece. There are two parts:* Song *and* Alborada.

SONG

Form and Key

Song is like a theme and ***variations*** with four sections:

A mm. 1-12
B mm. 13-20
C mm. 21-30
B_1 mm. 31-39

It is mainly in the ***Phrygian mode*** on E and has a definite modal sound (for example, in mm. 1-16).

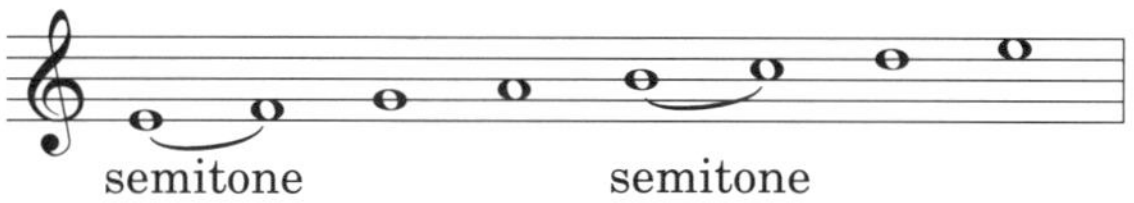

Takács uses a ***tonic pedal*** (E) throughout.

Metre

- *Song* is in 3/8, with a strong pulse on the first beat of each measure. The R.H. notes on the weak second beat (in mm. 1-12, 17-24, and 31-34) create a ***syncopated*** effect. Notice the contrast with the *espressivo* passages in mm. 13-16 and 25-30.
- Be generous with the *ritardando* and *fermata* in mm. 37-38 and hold the rest in m. 39 for its full value.

Articulation

- Make the *staccato* eighth notes short and consistent. Draw your finger in toward your palm as you release the key. Make the *staccato* quarter notes in mm. 1-6 a little longer.
- Play the *espressivo* passages with the padded part of your fingers. Aim for a warm, *cantabile* tone.
- Play the inverted ***mordents*** quickly but with expression.

ALBORADA

An *alborada* is a Spanish folk tune, played (or sung), often outside, at daybreak.

Form and Key

Alborada has three sections and a concluding fanfare:

D mm. 40-56
D_1 mm. 57-72
D mm. 73-87
fanfare mm. 88-95

It is mainly in A major with a ***dominant pedal***. Sometimes the tonic (A) appears with the pedal (for example in mm. 48-53). When the music ***modulates*** to C major in mm. 52-72, the pedal note is G.

In mm. 51-53 and 70-81, the L.H. plays an A major pedal (A-E) but the melody is in D major (notice the G natural in m. 53).

Metre and Rhythm

- *Alborada* moves more slowly than *Song* and is in a duple rather than a triple metre.
- The L.H. plays a percussive "drumbeat" accompaniment. Keep a steady pulse and play the rhythms precisely. Count in sixteenth notes.
- Think of clashing cymbals or a sharp drumbeat when you play the accented notes and ***sforzandos***. Play these notes with your fingertips.
- Hold the *tenuto* notes for their full value to emphasize them without an accent.
- In the final fanfare, the drumbeat takes over. Use all your strength for the *accelerando* and *crescendo* in the last three measures to give this piece a climactic finish.

Melody

- The sixteenth-note figure spinning out over the drumbeat accompaniment is related to the sixteenth-note ***motive*** in *Song*. Keep the sixteenth-note passages clear and even.
- This melody is marked "a little lazy." Use ***rubato*** to add expression. Let the tempo stretch and contract above the steady drumbeat in the L.H.

MARCH
OP. 65, NO. 10

List C: pp. 44-45

SERGEI PROKOFIEV (1891-1953)

Prokofiev showed early talent as both a pianist and a composer. He studied under Rimsky-Korsakov and others at the St. Petersburg Conservatory from the age of 13, and made a name for himself as an enfant terrible, *shocking everyone with his ultra-modern piano compositions. In 1917, he switched gears with his tuneful* Classical Symphony. *In the wake of the Russian Revolution (1917), he left his country and did not return until age 45. He spent the intervening years mainly in the United States and France. (For a brief period in 1920 he lived in Montreal.) In 1936, he returned to the Soviet Union, where he wrote some of his best loved music, including* Peter and The Wolf *(1936) and the ballet* Romeo and Juliet *(1938).*

March *is from* Music for Children, *a set of 12 piano pieces written in 1935. It is also one of seven pieces from this set orchestrated in 1941 to form the suite* Summer Day. *Prokofiev's unique piano style is often percussive and sharp, but it also has considerable melodic charm.*

A Two-Pulse Metre

Play this piece crisply and rhythmically. It is marked *tempo di marcia* (march tempo). Maintain a steady beat.

- The metronome marking is ♩ = 116-126. Although the time signature is 4/4, think of a pulse of two beats per measure. Stress the first beat and give the third beat a lighter accent.
- The accents marked in the music (for example, mm. 10, 16, and 18) are on the strong beats. (You might add a touch of pedal to the accents to enhance the tone.)
- The R.H. ***grace notes*** also emphasize the first and third beats. Play them quickly and cleanly, just before the beat.

Articulation

- Keep your fingers close to the keys for the *staccato* notes. This will give you greater control.
- Give the slurs an agile character. Play them with a bright sound and neatly clipped endings.

Dynamics

- Observe all the composer's dynamic markings. Without the contrast in dynamic levels, this piece would sound wooden and dry. The *crescendos* and *diminuendos* will help you to shape the music.
- Keep your arm relaxed to avoid a hard or forced tone in *forte* passages.

Crossing Hands

There is an awkward leap where the L.H. crosses the R.H. in mm. 12-15. Practise this shift of position by landing silently on the keys before you play them.

Play these notes firmly so that they ring out above the R.H. chords. The eighth-note rhythm is an important ***variation*** in the L.H. accompaniment pattern.

Form and Harmony

March has a two-measure introduction, followed by four sections:

A mm. 3-10
A_1 mm. 11-18
B mm. 18-26
A_2 mm. 27-34

Prokofiev's ***harmony*** is often quite modern and colourful, but the sequence of keys is rather conventional:

- Section A is in C major.
- In section A_1, the theme is ***transposed*** into F major (the ***subdominant*** key). In the final two measures, there is a ***modulation*** back to C major.
- Section B presents new material. The music hovers between A minor (the relative minor) and A major. The section ends on an A major chord.
- In section A_2, the main theme returns in the home key of C major.
- Compare the three A sections. What differences can you find?

PENTATONIC TUNE

List C: pp. 46-47

BÉLA BARTÓK (1881-1945)

Béla Bartók was born in Hungary. He gave his first concert at the age of 11. Later, he became a famous pianist, teacher and composer. Bartók was interested in folk music. He collected thousands of folk songs from Hungary, Romania, Ukraine, Bulgaria and Turkey. He was one of the first scholars to record and study this music. Pentatonic Tune *is from the first of a four-volume collection of piano pieces called* For Children.

The theme of this playful, energetic piece is a Hungarian folk song. Here are the words of the song:

Mother, dearest mother,
My boots are all worn out.
Who will finally mend them?

Pentatonic Scale

The melody is based on a ***pentatonic scale*** – that is, a scale which covers an octave in five notes. (Major and minor scales have seven pitches.) Here is the pentatonic scale that Bartók uses:

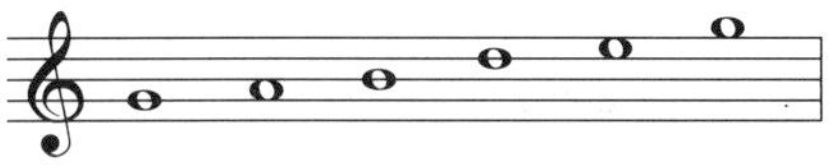

Form

This piece has two alternating themes – A and B. Here is the structure:

A	mm. 1-8
B	mm. 9-16
A_1	mm. 17-24
B_1	mm. 25-32
A_2	mm. 33-40
A+B	mm. 41-52
A_3	mm. 53-56

Repeating Themes

- A is an introduction or bridge passage. It begins as a tune but is dominated by one ***motive***.

  The A theme ends with a *poco ritardando*.
- In A_1, this motive is repeated two octaves higher with slightly different dynamics.
- In A_2, the L.H. plays an octave lower and the R.H. an octave higher. (The L.H. is marked *8va*. Play it one octave lower than written.)
- A_3 is a *coda* using only the A motive. Follow the *crescendo* to *mezzo forte* and don't slow down (*non ritardando*).
- The B theme is the folk-song melody. The L.H. plays the melody, and the R.H. plays off-beat chords. Project the melody and keep the *staccato* chords light. Each B section begins with an *a tempo*.
- In B_1, the melody is an octave lower and the R.H. plays continuous *staccato* chords. Notice that the L.H. is marked *mezzo piano* and the R.H., *piano*.
- In A+B (mm. 41-52), Bartók alternates two measures of B, played *piano*, with the motive from A, played *pianissimo*.

Articulation

Every note in this piece has an ***articulation*** mark.

1. Play the *staccato* notes crisply. Keep your fingers close to the keys.
2. Hold the *tenuto* notes for their full value, and give them a slight stress.
3. Play the accented notes firmly, and detach them a little. Take full advantage of the ***syncopated*** accent in m. 31.

Shifting Hand Position

In the R.H., m. 25, there is a quick shift of hand position.

Bounce lightly off the *staccato* G and move quickly down to the chord. Make sure your fingers are over the correct keys before you play the notes. Use the correct fingering. To practise this:

1. Play the G, then land silently on the chord slightly ahead of time.
2. Practise the position shift, allowing the chord to sound.
3. Practise the whole measure, keeping a steady tempo.

Allegro scherzando

Scherzo means joke. Keep this piece light and playful. In the A_3 section, imagine a jack-in-the-box or a cuckoo jumping out of a clock on the ***grace notes***.

FANTASIA

List C: page 48

PHILIPP JARNACH (1892-1982)

Jarnach was born in France. He studied at the Paris Conservatory from 1912 to 1914 and was in contact with Debussy and Ravel. At the outbreak of World War I, he moved to neutral Switzerland. In Zurich, he met and came under the influence of Ferruccio Busoni, the German-Italian composer and pianist. (Jarnach completed Busoni's last opera, Doktor Faust, *after Busoni's death in 1924.) In 1921 Jarnach moved to Berlin. Later he taught music in Cologne (1927-1949) and in Hamburg (1949-1970). His output includes chamber and instrumental works, orchestral pieces, and songs.*

Style

Fantasia has the quality of an improvisation. The music is based on the repetition and development of two ideas:

- The long, sustained chords played by the L.H.
- The rhapsodic, flowing, sixteenth-note figures in the melody.

The running melody and dark ***harmonies*** give this music the ***modal*** sound of Eastern-European folk music. Imagine this piece played by a small string orchestra, with a solo violinist playing the R.H. melody.

The R.H. and the L.H. part each have their own individual sound, and they often clash. The tension is not resolved until the final open 5th chord (C-G-G).

The Melody

Because the accidentals change frequently, there is no lasting sense of a key or mode. Instead, the melody circles around a fragment of one scale, then shifts to another.

- Don't rush this melody. Hold the longer notes for their full value. Give the sixteenth-note figures an elastic quality. Think of a hawk or an eagle soaring in the sky and moving along with an occasional wing beat.
- The sixteenth-note patterns are irregular. Find a comfortable fingering for each one and use it each time you practise.

The Accompaniment

The sustained sound and rhythmic punctuation in the L.H. provide an anchor for the melody.

- The chords are mostly open 5ths. Think of a bow being drawn across the open strings of a cello or contrabass.
- In mm. 3, 6, and 9-12, there is a dialogue between the hands. Let the L.H. speak as clearly and rhythmically as the R.H.

Rhythm and Metre

At first, you may find it difficult to sort out the rhythm from the maze of sixteenth notes. Mark the quarter-note beats in your music with dotted lines or arrows.

- Practise each dotted rhythm separately. Think in sixteenth notes.

- The frequent metre changes add to the improvisatory character of the music. Keep a steady quarter-note pulse, and stress the first beat of each measure.

7-10

  When you know the music, feel the rhythms in one-measure units (instead of one-beat units).
- In the last five measures, the dynamic level drops to *pianissimo*. Play softly but keep the dotted rhythms clear and precise.

Italian Terms

- *Recitando* is an Italian word meaning "like a recitative." A recitative is a vocal style which imitates the natural inflections of speech. Composers often use recitative in operas for the narrative text between arias.
- *Stringendo* means "tightening" or "narrowing." Here it indicates an increase of tempo, like an *accelerando*. Push the tempo ahead a little at the *stringendo* indications.
- From the beginning of your practising, include all the ***articulation***, dynamics, tempo changes, and "special effects" in the music. These details are just as important as the notes.

Pedal

Press the pedal down just a little. This will allow the strings to ring more freely. Change the pedal with the L.H. chords, but listen carefully, and add extra pedal changes to keep the sound from blurring.

GLOSSARY OF TERMS

accelerando (accel.)
becoming faster

accent
stressed note [>]

acciaccatura
see ***grace note***

accidental
a sharp, flat or natural sign in front of a note. An accidental affects a note for only one measure; it is cancelled by a bar line.

Alberti bass
a L.H. broken-chord accompaniment pattern

appoggiatura
an ***ornament*** played on a strong beat

articulation
the way in which notes are played: long or short, separated (detached, *staccato*) or joined together (*legato*). *See also marcato, portato, tenuto.*

auxiliary note
a ***non-chord tone***, one degree higher or lower than the note of the chord (also called a neighbour note)

binary form
a structure of two sections (AB), both of which may be repeated. In **rounded binary form**, the B section ends with a partial repeat of A.

bridge
a connecting passage between two main themes or sections

cadence
two or more chords used at the end of a phrase, section, or composition. A **perfect cadence** moves from a ***dominant*** chord to ***tonic*** chord (V-I). An **imperfect cadence** moves from a ***tonic*** chord to ***dominant*** chord (I-V). A **deceptive cadence** moves from a ***dominant*** or a ***supertonic*** chord to ***submediant*** chord (V-VI or II-VI).

canon
a technique in which a melody is stated in one part or voice, and strictly ***imitated*** in one or more parts

cantabile
in a singing style

chord
three or more notes sounding together

chromatic
use of notes outside of, or in addition to, the usual degrees of a major or minor scale

coda (codetta)
a concluding section added to the basic form. (In Italian, *coda* means "tail.") A *codetta* is a little *coda*.

counterpoint (adj. contrapuntal)
two or more melodic lines or voices, sounding at the same time

degrees of the scale
the names and numerals that designate the notes of a major or minor scale:
I ***tonic***
II ***supertonic***
III ***mediant***
IV ***subdominant***
V ***dominant***
VI ***submediant***
VII **leading note**

detached
short, but not as short as *staccato*

development
see ***sonata form***

diminished 7th
a four-note chord built of minor 3rds (B-D-F-A flat)

dissonance
notes sounding together that produce a relatively harsh or discordant sound

dominant
the fifth degree of a scale

dominant 7th
a ***dominant*** chord with added minor 7th (C-E-G-B flat)

downbeat
the first beat of the measure

drone
long, sustained sound, normally a bass note

dynamics
variations in the volume of sound, expressed by terms and signs such as:
crescendo (cresc.) [<] become louder
decrescendo (decresc.) [>] become softer
diminuendo (dim.) diminish
fortissimo (ff) very loud
forte (f) loud
mezzo forte (mf) moderately loud
mezzo piano (mp) moderately soft
piano (p) soft
pianissimo (pp) very soft

exposition
see ***sonata form***

fermata
a pause

forzando
forced, accented

grace note
note played before the beat; printed in small type and usually slurred to the note it ***ornaments***

harmony
the chordal, or vertical, structure of music (in contrast to the melodic, or horizontal, structure)

hemiola
the proportion of two to three. In the 16th century this term was used to describe a pattern of two against three. Later, *hemiola* was used to refer to a change in rhythm where two measures of triple time are made to sound like three measures of duple time, or vice versa.

imitation
exact repetition of one part or voice at another pitch; non-exact repetition is called "free imitation"

interval
the distance in pitch between two tones. The name of each interval indicates the number of tones of the major (or minor) scale it includes.

inversion
the reversal of a pattern or interval (turning upside down, mirror image)

legato
smoothly

marcato
marked or stressed

mediant
the third degree of a scale

mode
a type of scale that gives a special flavour to music. Modes are the basis for much church music, folk music and jazz. Some modes are:
Aeolian: white notes from A to A
Dorian: white notes from D to D
Lydian: white notes from F to F
Phrygian: white notes from E to E

modulation
a change of key

mordent
an ***ornament*** consisting of the alternation of the written note with the note below

motive
a small unit or figure, either melodic or rhythmic

non-chord tone
a tone that does not belong to the ***harmony*** (i.e., to the chord) but which adds melodic interest. *See also* ***appoggiatura*** and ***auxiliary note***.

off-beat
on a weak beat or a weak part of a beat

ornament
note, or notes, added to the melody for decoration

ostinato
a persistently repeated ***motive*** or phrase

pedal (or pedal point)
long-held note (normally the ***tonic*** or the ***dominant***) in any voice but usually in the bass

phrase
a short passage, often of two to four measures

pivot chord
a chord common to the ***harmony*** of two keys used to move from one key to the other in a ***modulation***

poco
a little

portato
halfway between *staccato* and *legato*

rallentando (rall.); ritardando (rit.)
slowing down

recapitulation
see ***sonata form***

rinforzando (rfz.)
strongly accented

ritenuto (riten.)
slowing down suddenly

rondo form
a form in which a recurring theme alternates with one or more contrasting themes (ABACA)

rubato
an elastic, flexible tempo using slight variations of speed to enhance musical expression

scale
a collection of pitches arranged in a particular order; a ***chromatic*** scale moves by semitones; a **whole-tone** scale moves by whole tones; a **pentatonic** scale has five pitches

sequence
repetition of a ***motive*** at a different pitch

sforzando (sfz)
strongly accented

slur
small group of notes under a curved line which is played *legato*

sonata (sonatina)
a work for one or more solo instruments, usually in several movements; a sonatina is a little sonata

sonata form
form of an extended movement of a sonata, with three main sections:
- an **exposition**, in which two keys are contrasted with each other, often by means of separate, contrasting themes
- a **development**, in which themes from the exposition are varied and re-worked
- a **recapitulation**, in which the themes from the exposition are restated in the tonic key
- a ***coda*** is often added to conclude the movement

sostenuto
sustained

staccato
very short

subdominant
the fourth degree of a scale

submediant
the sixth degree of a scale

suite
a group of dance movements, often in the same key

supertonic
the second degree of a scale

syncopation
a shifting of the normal beat or accent, resulting in an emphasis on the weak beat

tenuto
hold a note for its full value

ternary form
a structure of three sections (ABA) in which B is a contrast to A. The repeat of A can be a little different.

tièrce de Picardie (Picardy 3rd)
a major chord at the end of a piece in a minor key

tonic
the first degree of a scale

transposition
playing or writing music in a key that is different from the original

triad
a chord of three pitches, arranged in 3rds

trill

an ***ornament*** consisting of the rapid alternation between a note and the note above

triplet

three notes played in the time of two

turn

an ***ornament*** of four or five notes that turn around the principal note

upbeat

note or group of notes beginning a phrase on the weak beat (or weak part of the beat), just before the bar line

variation

a repetition of a ***motive*** or theme with changes – the changes can be slight or significant

voice leading

the progression of individual voices in a multi-voiced texture